FLEXIBLESPACES

A FRANK BETZ ASSOCIATES INC. COLLECTION

728.37
FLEX
c.1

FRANK BETZ
INTRODUCTION

Beautiful homes begin with curb appeal and a striking presentation to the streetscape, yet the true beauty of a house lies within its four walls. It is with this in mind that Frank Betz Associates presents this group of plans that allow us to choose how we use the spaces provided to us. The way we use these spaces tells the story of our lives and families. Whether a loft is used as an office or play-room helps define where our priorities lie. A 21st-century element revisited from ages past is the keeping room, an informal space that invites family gatherings as well as individual pursuits, such as reading, planning and browsing the Internet.

These flexible designs inspire the homeowner to think beyond today and envision how their lives will change tomorrow. Inside these pages are plans that offer flexible spaces, including keeping rooms, lofts, optional bedrooms, bonus rooms and home offices. Browse, enjoy and dream of plans for today, tomorrow and beyond. ■

Left | Coursed fieldstone on the walls contrast with random stone on the porch floor creating an interesting effect.

CONTENTS

Left | An arched cased opening provides entry to a warm family area.

A DESIGNS DIRECT PUBLISHING BOOK

presented by

FRANK
BETZ
ASSOCIATES
INC.

Betz Publishing, LLC.
2401 Lake Park Drive, Suite 250
Smyrna, GA 30080
888.717.3003 | www.flexiblespaces.com

Floor plans and elevations are subject to change. Floor plan dimensions are approximate. Consult working drawings for actual dimensions and information. Elevations are artists' conceptions.

Frank Betz – *President*

Laura Segers – *Editor-in-Chief*

Russell Moody – *Editor*

Martha Stalvey – *Editor*

Allen Bennetts – *Illustrator*

Joshua Thomas – *Art Director*

Contributing Writers – Laura Hurst Brown, Sarah Hockman

Contributing Photographers – Happy Terrebone/Happy Terrebone Photography, Visual Solutions, Bryan Willy/Bryan Willy Photography

Prepress services by DMG Inc., Atlanta
Printed by Toppan Printing Company, Hong Kong

ISBN   1 - 9 3 2 5 5 3 - 0 5 - 3

First Printing, September 2004

From top left to bottom right |
Bead-board wainscoting along with warm fabrics create a warm, cozy room.

Deep green walls give this bedroom a peaceful feeling.

Sunlight fills this spacious living area.

Keeping rooms such as this are sure to be a favorite space for the family.

The vaulted ceiling finished with beams and tongue-and-groove wood adds volume to this living room.

Moody Residence (pages 8 to 13) evokes the charm of Southern vernaculars yet steps into the future with sensational amenities.

Left | Plush fabrics complement a palette of earthen hues and masonry in a sitting area that owns a sense of intimacy.

Right | A winding stair case links public and private realms and visually integrates the heart of the home.

DESIGN
PHILOSOPHY OF
FLEXIBLE
SPACES

Decades after Boomtown USA swept across the nation—leaving in its wake myriad clusters of boxy burbs—we are rethinking the urban strategy. No longer willing to settle for hodgepodge communities of houses with bare-bones character and few links to the past, today's designers take on the future with ergonomic footprints drawn to both maximize function and tap into a diverse repertoire of time-honored vocabularies. Rich with updated architectural accoutrements and fresh mixes of tactile materials and trim lines, these homes demonstrate the suitability of new-century styles for young, modern families.

Textured elevations of brick and stucco, clapboard and stone announce stylish, livable interiors with hardworking rooms that maintain the charm of gentler times. Powerhouse blends of curb appeal and comfort create real-world retreats with flexible floor plans that are fully prepared for change and deceptively smart on space. Living areas that flex from formal to casual and old-new spaces, such as keeping rooms, redefine our notions of how houses respond to uncommonly busy and complex lifestyles. Open-plan kitchens equipped with shiny 21st-century appliances and hand-crafted cabinetry overlook informal gathering zones that serve many functions.

Great rooms not only flex to facilitate family gatherings, jigsaw puzzles and movie nights, they easily convert to sun rooms, cyber-game spaces and home offices. Rows of windows and French doors illuminate these casual zones with natural light and scenery, while decks, porticos and porches extend living spaces and invite the pleasures of lingering. Advanced electronics coexist

Above | Natural materials add texture and definition to open, flexible areas that adapt to many occasions.

Right | Deeply comfortable game rooms provide respite from the more formal spaces in the home.

with rough-hewn stone hearth surrounds and beamed ceilings, seamlessly integrating the best of what's gone before with the tomorrow-esque requirements of day-to-day life.

Deeply comfortable guest spaces complement bonus rooms that adapt to the changing needs of a family's lifetime. Easily developed to accommodate a nanny, maid or live-in relative, a secluded space can evolve to provide privacy for a teenager or returning college student. Later, the room becomes a game room or craft center. And at any time during the course of a family's growth, this vital flex area can provide personal space—a quiet place that serves as a meditative retreat, yoga or exercise room, or kick-back area strewn with books and favorite magazines.

Computer lofts and libraries, ateliers and planning centers are the new must-have spaces in home design, and open arrangements of spaces that readily give up their id's to enhance the function and pump up the livability of a plan are top drawer. Never mind that there are no rooms that simply sit unused for years—the homes in this collection incorporate cutting-edge capabilities with the craftsmanship and quality of ages past. Here are houses tuned to the future, with highly flexible rooms, superbly designed and ready to build in any region. Unrestrained and spacious, these designs capture a vocabulary of adaptable spaces and open rooms that fit modern lifestyles perfectly.

Left | Luxe mixes of leather, wood and fabric confront 21st-century technology in a splendid home theater.

Above | A home office retreat can take on the very individual character of its owner.

Left | Flower colors pop up everywhere in a little girl's room that is prepared for change as the child grows.

Right | Tray ceiling treatments add definition to open spaces and lend a sense of adventure.

FLEXIBLE SPACES
THAT CHANGE WITH TIME

Houses of the 21st-Century satisfy many generations of homeowners with diverse lifestyles in myriad phases of growth. Some owners are just starting to think about what their first home might look like; others are shopping for a seasonal place to fit their vision of paradise. Owners whose children have grown and gone on to start families of their own enjoy solitude, while a home with no children and two breadwinners often yields to a highly functional environment. Families with young, growing children require a house to adapt quickly to life changes, with rooms that can one year be a nursery, then au pair quarters, and finally a study or library. A mature family may need to develop the bonus space over the garage into a teenager's room or student's quarters, or to convert a main-level room to accommodate a live-in grandparent.

The common element—one that every homeowner shares—is a desire to find a place designed for the well-lived life. A house that is perfectly suited to its owners provides public spaces luxe enough to host a savory soiree yet practical enough for pets and bare feet. Owners also want a place to retreat, a personal space that is just right for browsing favorite books and magazines, catching up on the news, practicing yoga or pulling thirty minutes on the treadmill. A bit of privacy for the kids may mean an upper game or recreation room, or a secluded wing to help buffer the amps on a new electric guitar.

Rooms that flex and change according to their owners' preferences and adapt to their needs are vital to the scheme of the whole house. A half century ago, worthwhile designs featured separate formal living and dining rooms toward the front of the plan—typically reserved for guests and traditional

Above Left | Natural rough-hewn materials set a mood and establish an identity for a space that flexes over time.

Above Right | An entry hall employs ebonized furnishings and balusters to anchor an airy space that leads to the public realm.

Right | A coffered ceiling echoes the linear pattern of a row of windows in a grand great room.

gatherings—with bedrooms and casual spaces to the rear of the home, and halls to link them to the public zone. Today, foyers extend the function of the entry and front porch by creating an easy transition from the streetscape to open arrangements of rooms that fluctuate from high glam to family-only gatherings. Kitchens are the center of gravity in these homes, with food-prep islands that overlook conversation groupings, wrapping counters and wide snack bars for on-the-go salads and sandwiches. Great rooms open to spectacular views and outside spaces that further the livability of the heart of the home. And new versions of familiar places, such as lofts and keeping rooms, are the must-haves of today's savvy home builder.

KEEPING ROOMS

In Colonial houses, the plan provided only one room, and that was the keeping room. Of course, this space served a multitude of purposes, and the family prepared meals, ate and worked there. And at day's end, the grownups and infants slept near the warm hearth, while the older children slept in the attic. Today, brand new plans redefine this versatile space as an informal extension of the kitchen and morning room. Smaller and cozier than the great room, the 21st-century keeping room maintains a casual, intimate spirit yet takes on advanced functions, such as harboring the home's cyber center and media systems. A great example of a keeping room that enhances the casual living zone is the Westhampton [page 32]. Rough-hewn timber beams lend a human scale to the vaulted ceilings, fireplaces add warmth and character, and walls of glass bring in views and a sense of nature. Tray and coffered ceilings refine the palette and add a sense of space while maintaining the proportions of the room.

BONUS ROOMS

Perhaps the most popular flex space in today's home is the bonus room. Originally created in midcentury homes to capture the space under the rooflines and employed as a rough-cut attic or atelier, today's upper-level bonus spaces offer homeowners a virtually

Right | A window seat defines the perimeter of this morning room, while a set of French doors help illuminate the space.

unlimited menu of options for development. In larger homes, the bonus room is situated above the garage and offers enough square footage for a home theater or media center. Or the space can flex to a recreation area, a reading room or a place for computers. Kids can go there to let off steam or study for the next exam. A great example of a plan with flexible space for children is the Woodcliffe [page 40]: the upper level features a three-step-up recreation room that complements a spacious unfinished area with wide windows.

HOME OFFICES

Every well-equipped home must have a home office, in the same way that older homes required a parlor or library. Although this space rarely serves as a gathering area, the office is essential as a planning center for the household. Built-in cabinetry and ample space for computers provide a sense of scale and intimacy—important considerations especially when the office is situated in the public realm. Privacy is maintained by double or French doors, which, when open, permit a fluid arrangement with the foyer. If the room is also command central for a home-based business, then its strategic location within the plan is even more vital. Placed near the front or side entry, the room offers unfettered access for both clients and guests, and often adjoins a full bath and includes a wardrobe or closet, which permit an easy conversion to guest quarters. Because the home office is primarily positioned near the master suite, this space could also serve as a convenient nursery.

Left | Vintage décor subdues a high-volume space that easily converts to guest quarters.

Above | A home office provides the ultimate connection between function and style.

LOFT SPACES

More than any other type of flexible space in modern homes, lofts infuse the plans with a spirit of fun. The mere mention of the word calls up visions of play and idiosyncratic spaces that seem to allow one the ease of a distant perspective. Even very traditional lofts with formal arrangements of desks and upholstered chairs provide owners with a visionary perspective above the public realm or great room. Shapely balusters or stair rails visually separate the loft from the main level, but the spatial links to the upper and lower rooms are vital connections within the home. A flex space that is as comfortable as a conversation spot as it is as study area, the loft holds an infinite capacity for change as the family's needs evolve. Located near a cluster of secondary bedrooms, the space invites kids to gather for talk or cyber games. Later, the loft harbors homework and books for a college student, or becomes a craft space for the owners.

GAME ROOMS

Typically situated either above or below the main level, game rooms provide an ultra-comfortable space for family members to gather. Bonus rooms and basements can convert to these recreational spaces, or they can grow to elaborate lower-level areas that include a full kitchen, a wet bar, a casual eating area and perhaps a bath.

This collection of plans speaks volumes about the ways in which we live today. The homes are less formal, more progressive and clearly more flexible than the houses our parents grew up in, although some of the familiar amenities can be found here too: formal dining rooms link to the pantry or serving areas of kitchens, natural selections of wood and stone look great together, and fireplaces tame the scale of the central living rooms. Here are hardworking designs that infuse their thoroughly modern interiors with a satisfying spirit of comfort and style. ■

Left | Rugged materials serve to unify spacious, flex areas with the rustic elements of the house.

KEEPING ROOMS

Houses with keeping rooms epitomize the highly developed standards for flexibility in today's home. Derived from colonial vernaculars, in which early designs set the standard for facilitating multiple tasks, this versatile space handles many of the family's requirements for every-day life. For example, the keeping room can take on computers, sewing machines, craft tables, and media stations. More than just a gathering zone, the keeping room employs a palette of comfortable textures and furnishings in order to create a place that invites get-togethers and individual pursuits. The Flanagan [page 54] adapts to changing lifestyles by keeping an open relationship between the kitchen, breakfast room and keeping room—one that allows all of the areas to share the warmth and character of a centered fireplace—and permits the function of the space to change over time. For young families, it is a playroom; while for couples in retirement, the space becomes a reading or craft room. And while the mood of the space is typically simple, the architectural details can be very rich and detailed. ■

Left | Corinthian columns form the fireplace surround to create the focal point of this room.

© Frank Betz Associates, Inc.

DEVONHURST

The columns along the front covered porch of this lovely home make for a distinguished, elegant entrance. The vaulted family room forms the centerpiece of the living space, featuring a warm, inviting fireplace. A vaulted keeping room adjoins the breakfast area.   The main floor is also home to the master suite and bath, and two additional bedrooms. Upstairs, there's plenty of room for a fourth bedroom as well as children's retreat.

Rear Elevation

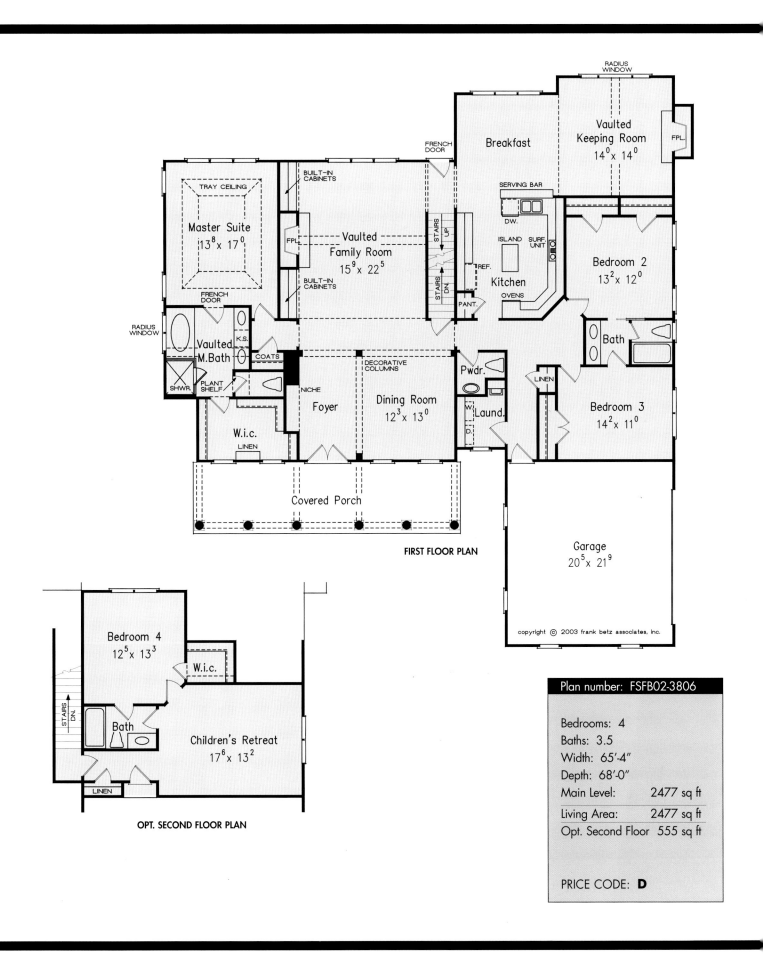

FIRST FLOOR PLAN

TRAY CEILING

Master Suite
13⁸ x 17⁰

BUILT-IN CABINETS

FRENCH DOOR

Vaulted Family Room
15⁹ x 22⁵

BUILT-IN CABINETS

FPL

RADIUS WINDOW

Vaulted M.Bath

K.S.

COATS

SHWR.

PLANT SHELF

W.i.c.

LINEN

NICHE

Foyer

DECORATIVE COLUMNS

Dining Room
12³ x 13⁰

STAIRS UP

STAIRS DN

PANT.

REF.

Pwdr.

Laund.
W.
D.

Covered Porch

Breakfast

RADIUS WINDOW

Vaulted Keeping Room
14⁰ x 14⁰

FPL

SERVING BAR

DW.

ISLAND

SURF. UNIT

Kitchen

OVENS

Bedroom 2
13² x 12⁰

Bath

LINEN

Bedroom 3
14² x 11⁰

Garage
20⁵ x 21⁹

copyright © 2003 frank betz associates, inc.

OPT. SECOND FLOOR PLAN

Bedroom 4
12⁵ x 13³

W.i.c.

STAIRS DN

Bath

Children's Retreat
17⁶ x 13²

LINEN

Plan number: FSFB02-3806

Bedrooms: 4
Baths: 3.5
Width: 65'-4"
Depth: 68'-0"
Main Level: 2477 sq ft
Living Area: 2477 sq ft
Opt. Second Floor 555 sq ft

PRICE CODE: **D**

KEEPING ROOMS

GREYTHORNE

Rear Elevation

Thoughtful and creative design makes the Greythorne unique in both the layout and the details. The full-service kitchen has an attention-grabbing coffered ceiling. Adjoining this room is a vaulted keeping room. Accessible from both the master suite and the keeping room is a covered back porch – a quiet place to retreat after a busy day. Window seats are incorporated into the master suite and the fourth bedroom.

TO ORDER PLANS CALL TOLL FREE 888-717-3003

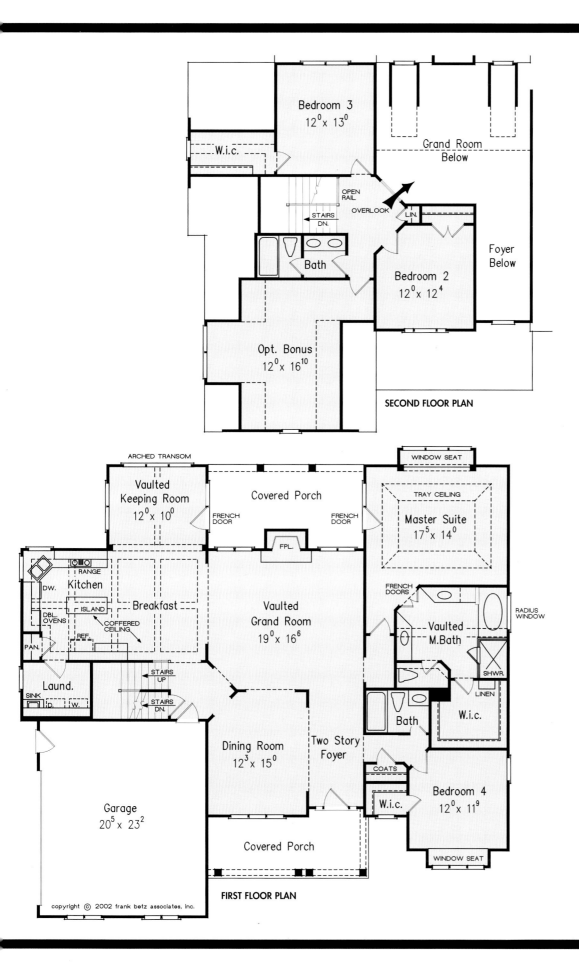

Bedroom 3
12⁰ x 13⁰

Grand Room
Below

W.i.c.

OPEN RAIL

OVERLOOK

STAIRS DN.

LIN.

Foyer Below

Bath

Bedroom 2
12⁰ x 12⁴

Opt. Bonus
12⁰ x 16¹⁰

SECOND FLOOR PLAN

Plan number: FSFB02-3764

Bedrooms: 4
Baths: 3
Width: 60'-0"
Depth: 56'-0"
Main Level: 2047 sq ft
Upper Level: 540 sq ft

Living Area: 2587 sq ft
Opt. Bonus Room 278 sq ft

PRICE CODE: **E**

ARCHED TRANSOM

Vaulted
Keeping Room
12⁰ x 10⁰

FRENCH DOOR

Covered Porch

FRENCH DOOR

WINDOW SEAT

TRAY CEILING

Master Suite
17⁵ x 14⁰

FPL.

RANGE

Kitchen

DW.

DBL. OVENS

ISLAND

Breakfast

COFFERED CEILING

REF.

Vaulted
Grand Room
19⁰ x 16⁶

FRENCH DOORS

Vaulted
M.Bath

RADIUS WINDOW

PAN.

STAIRS UP

SHWR.

LINEN

Laund.

SINK

D.

W.

STAIRS DN.

W.i.c.

Dining Room
12³ x 15⁰

Two Story
Foyer

Bath

COATS

W.i.c.

Bedroom 4
12⁰ x 11⁹

Garage
20⁵ x 23²

Covered Porch

WINDOW SEAT

copyright © 2002 frank betz associates, inc.

FIRST FLOOR PLAN

ROSEMORE PLACE

Distinctive fieldstone and cedar shake give the façade of the Rosemore Place warm texture and dimension. This warmth radiates inside as well with a fire-lit keeping room just off the kitchen. The master suite is private and secluded on the main level of the home. A private sitting area personalizes this space. The main floor bedroom can act as the home office-perfect for the telecommuter or entrepreneur. An optional bonus room is designed for the upper floor with endless possibilities – a fifth bedroom, recreation room, or fitness area would all be easily accommodated by this space.

Rear Elevation

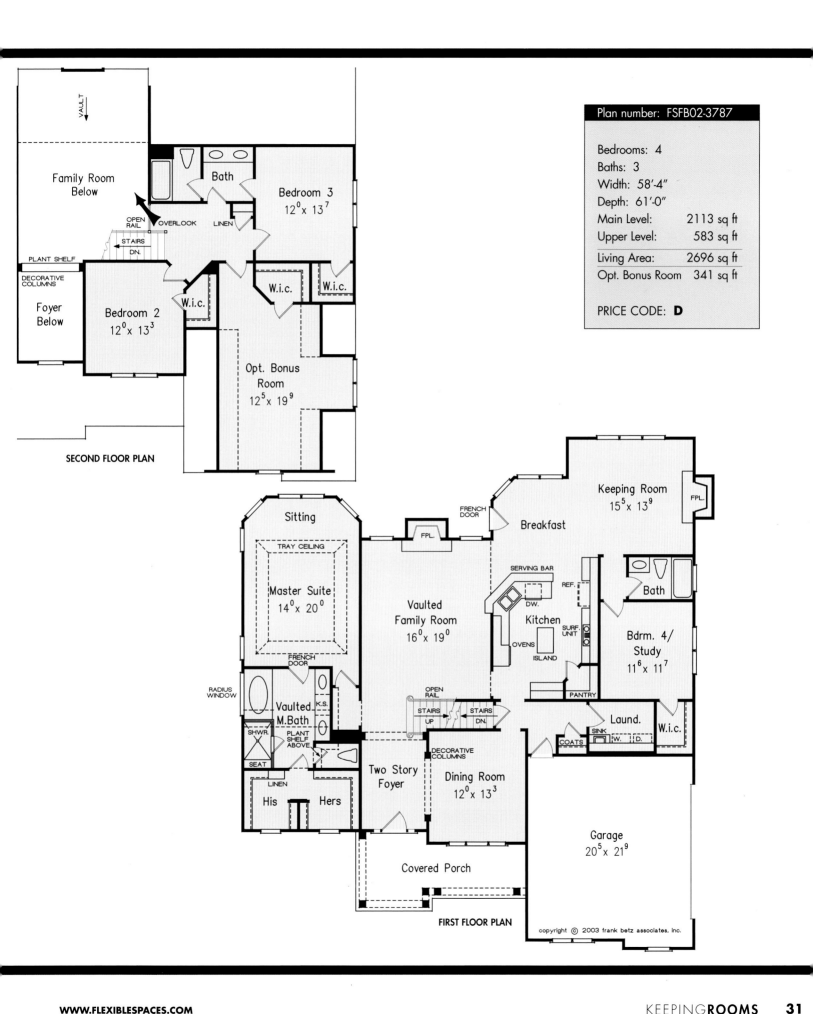

VAULT

Family Room Below

Bath

Bedroom 3
12⁰ x 13⁷

OPEN RAIL OVERLOOK LINEN

STAIRS DN.

PLANT SHELF

DECORATIVE COLUMNS

Foyer Below

Bedroom 2
12⁰ x 13³

W.i.c.

W.i.c.

W.i.c.

Opt. Bonus Room
12⁵ x 19⁹

SECOND FLOOR PLAN

Plan number: FSFB02-3787

Bedrooms: 4
Baths: 3
Width: 58'-4"
Depth: 61'-0"
Main Level: 2113 sq ft
Upper Level: 583 sq ft
Living Area: 2696 sq ft
Opt. Bonus Room   341 sq ft

PRICE CODE: **D**

Sitting

TRAY CEILING

Master Suite
14⁰ x 20⁰

FRENCH DOOR

FRENCH DOOR

Breakfast

Keeping Room
15⁵ x 13⁹

FPL.

FPL.

SERVING BAR

REF.

DW.

Bath

Vaulted Family Room
16⁰ x 19⁰

Kitchen

SURF. UNIT

OVENS

ISLAND

Bdrm. 4/ Study
11⁶ x 11⁷

RADIUS WINDOW

Vaulted M.Bath

K.S.

PANTRY

SHWR.

PLANT SHELF ABOVE

SEAT

OPEN RAIL

STAIRS UP

STAIRS DN.

Laund.

W.i.c.

COATS

SINK

W. D.

LINEN

His

Hers

Two Story Foyer

DECORATIVE COLUMNS

Dining Room
12⁰ x 13³

Garage
20⁵ x 21⁹

Covered Porch

FIRST FLOOR PLAN

copyright © 2003 frank betz associates, inc.

WESTHAMPTON

Rear Elevation

The distinctive stone exterior of the Westhampton sets the stage for the unique layout inside. A cozy keeping room is situated adjacent to the kitchen, creating uncommon angles rarely found in stock home plans. A third garage bay is separate from the others, providing the perfect spot for boat or utility storage. Three upstairs bedrooms feature generous dimensions and private access to bathing areas. The master suite boasts a bayed sitting area.

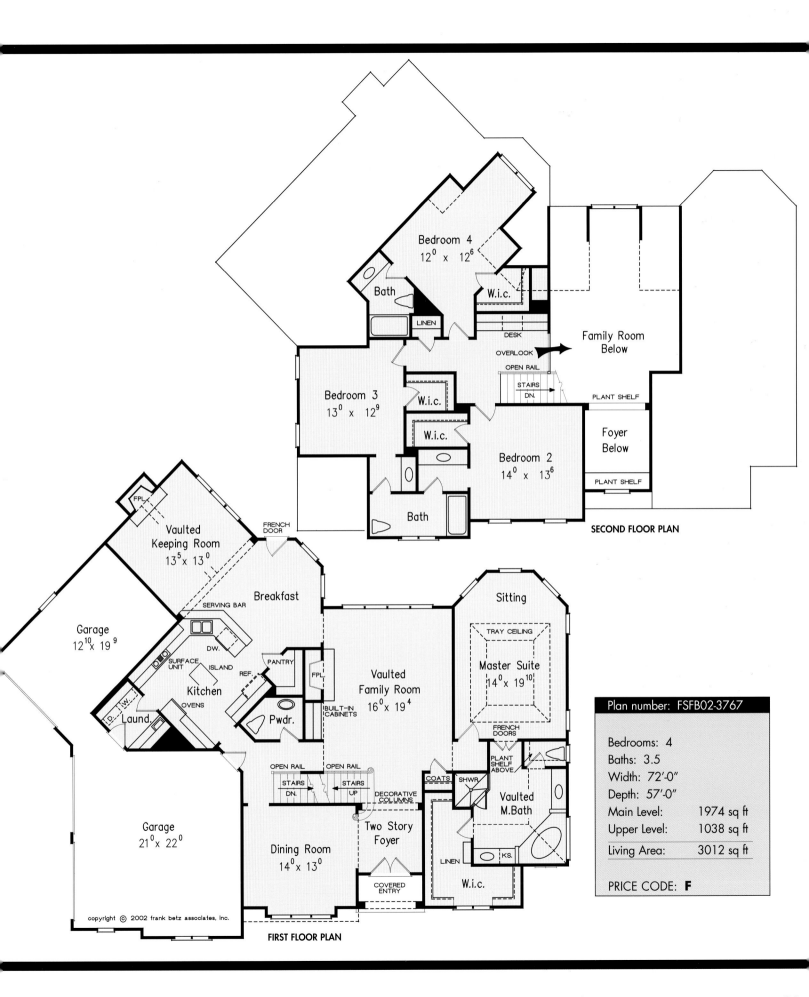

Bedroom 4
$12^0 \times 12^6$

Bath

W.i.c.

LINEN

DESK

Family Room Below

OVERLOOK

OPEN RAIL

STAIRS DN.

PLANT SHELF

Bedroom 3
$13^0 \times 12^9$

W.i.c.

W.i.c.

Foyer Below

Bath

Bedroom 2
$14^0 \times 13^6$

PLANT SHELF

SECOND FLOOR PLAN

FPL.

Vaulted Keeping Room
$13^5 \times 13^0$

FRENCH DOOR

Breakfast

SERVING BAR

Sitting

TRAY CEILING

Garage
$12^{10} \times 19^9$

DW.

SURFACE UNIT

ISLAND

REF.

PANTRY

FPL

Vaulted Family Room
$16^0 \times 19^4$

Master Suite
$14^0 \times 19^{10}$

Kitchen

OVENS

Pwdr.

BUILT-IN CABINETS

FRENCH DOORS

D. W.

Laund.

PLANT SHELF ABOVE

OPEN RAIL

OPEN RAIL

COATS

SHWR

Vaulted M.Bath

STAIRS DN.

STAIRS UP

DECORATIVE COLUMNS

Garage
$21^0 \times 22^0$

Two Story Foyer

LINEN

W.S.

Dining Room
$14^0 \times 13^0$

W.i.c.

COVERED ENTRY

FIRST FLOOR PLAN

Plan number: FSFB02-3767

Bedrooms: 4
Baths: 3.5
Width: 72'-0"
Depth: 57'-0"
Main Level: 1974 sq ft
Upper Level: 1038 sq ft
Living Area: 3012 sq ft

PRICE CODE: **F**

© Frank Betz Associates, Inc.

LAUREL RIVER

Rear Elevation

The space in this ranch is unbelievable! Few ranch plans can boast the square footage and amenities that this one provides. The impressive master suite has spacious his and her closets and a sitting room, perfect for relaxing. This split bedroom layout allows for an additional guest bedroom. A spacious kitchen and breakfast room are complemented by a vaulted keeping room, adorned with its own fireplace. The vaulted grand room with fireplace and built-in bookcases adds a nice touch of grandeur.

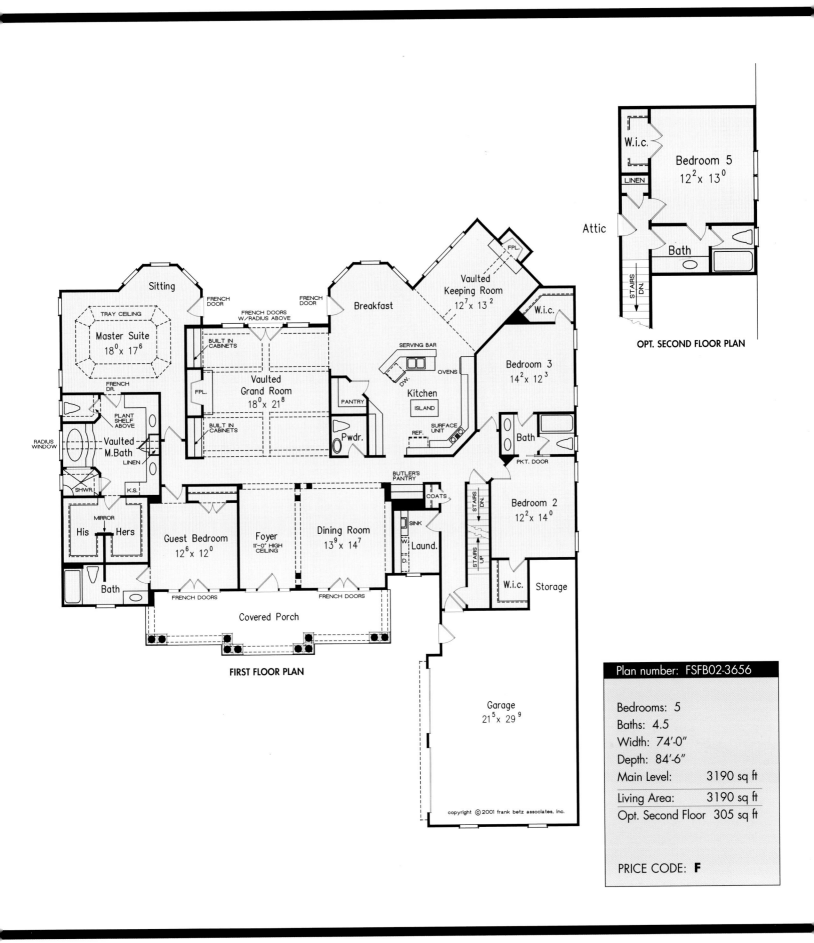

Sitting

TRAY CEILING

Master Suite
18⁰ x 17⁶

FRENCH DR.

FRENCH DOOR

FRENCH DOORS W/RADIUS ABOVE

FRENCH DOOR

Breakfast

FPL.

Vaulted Keeping Room
12⁷ x 13²

W.i.c.

PLANT SHELF ABOVE

BUILT IN CABINETS

Vaulted Grand Room
18⁰ x 21⁸

FPL.

SERVING BAR

DW.

OVENS

Bedroom 3
14² x 12³

RADIUS WINDOW

Vaulted M.Bath

LINEN

PANTRY

BUILT IN CABINETS

Kitchen

ISLAND

REF.

SURFACE UNIT

Bath

SHWR.

K.S.

Pwdr.

PKT. DOOR

MIRROR

His **Hers**

Bath

Guest Bedroom
12⁶ x 12⁰

Foyer
11'-0" HIGH CEILING

Dining Room
13⁹ x 14⁷

BUTLER'S PANTRY

COATS

SINK

W. D.

Laund.

STAIRS DN.

Bedroom 2
12² x 14⁰

STAIRS UP

W.i.c. **Storage**

FRENCH DOORS

FRENCH DOORS

Covered Porch

FIRST FLOOR PLAN

Garage
21⁵ x 29⁹

copyright © 2001 frank betz associates, inc.

W.i.c.

Attic

LINEN

Bedroom 5
12² x 13⁰

STAIRS DN.

Bath

OPT. SECOND FLOOR PLAN

Plan number: FSFB02-3656

Bedrooms: 5

Baths: 4.5

Width: 74'-0"

Depth: 84'-6"

Main Level: 3190 sq ft

Living Area: 3190 sq ft

Opt. Second Floor 305 sq ft

PRICE CODE: **F**

FORREST HILLS

The façade of this lovely Southern home features a charming mix of beautiful roofing, siding and window detailing. The front door leads into a two-story foyer brightly lit by a large window above. Upstairs, three bedrooms overlook a warm, inviting family room. The island kitchen leads to a breakfast bay and vaulted keeping room, which looks onto the backyard.

Rear Elevation

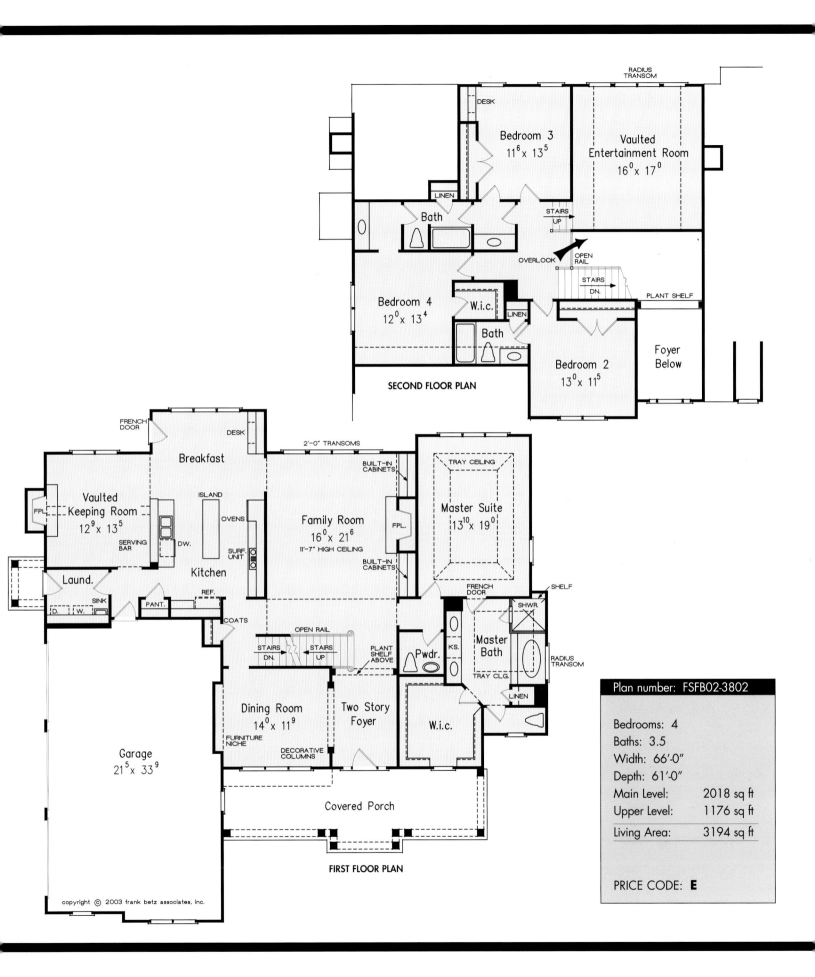

SECOND FLOOR PLAN

RADIUS TRANSOM

DESK

Bedroom 3
11⁶ x 13⁵

Vaulted Entertainment Room
16⁰ x 17⁰

LINEN

Bath

STAIRS UP

OPEN RAIL

OVERLOOK

STAIRS DN.

PLANT SHELF

Bedroom 4
12⁰ x 13⁴

W.i.c.

LINEN

Bath

Foyer Below

Bedroom 2
13⁰ x 11⁵

FIRST FLOOR PLAN

FRENCH DOOR

Breakfast

DESK

2'-0" TRANSOMS

BUILT-IN CABINETS

TRAY CEILING

FPL.

Vaulted Keeping Room
12⁹ x 13⁵

ISLAND

OVENS

Family Room
16⁰ x 21⁶
11'-7" HIGH CEILING

FPL.

Master Suite
13¹⁰ x 19⁰

SERVING BAR

DW.

SURF. UNIT

BUILT-IN CABINETS

Laund.

Kitchen

SINK

PANT.

REF.

COATS

FRENCH DOOR

SHELF

SHWR.

Master Bath

RADIUS TRANSOM

D. W.

OPEN RAIL

STAIRS DN.

STAIRS UP

PLANT SHELF ABOVE

Pwdr.

KS.

LINEN

TRAY CLG.

Dining Room
14⁰ x 11⁹

Two Story Foyer

W.i.c.

Garage
21⁵ x 33⁹

FURNITURE NICHE

DECORATIVE COLUMNS

Covered Porch

copyright © 2003 frank betz associates, inc.

Plan number: FSFB02-3802	
Bedrooms:	4
Baths:	3.5
Width:	66'-0"
Depth:	61'-0"
Main Level:	2018 sq ft
Upper Level:	1176 sq ft
Living Area:	3194 sq ft

PRICE CODE: **E**

KENTHURST

This masterpiece is full of pleasant surprises. A beautiful covered porch on the front of the home makes a wonderful entrance. A secondary covered entrance is placed near the garage bays and leads directly to the laundry room, keeping clutter in its place. A striking keeping room is connected to the kitchen, featuring a fireplace, built-in cabinetry and vaulted ceilings. Homeowners will appreciate the master suite's private sitting area when it comes time to rest for the evening. The main floor fifth bedroom also makes an ideal location for a study.

Rear Elevation

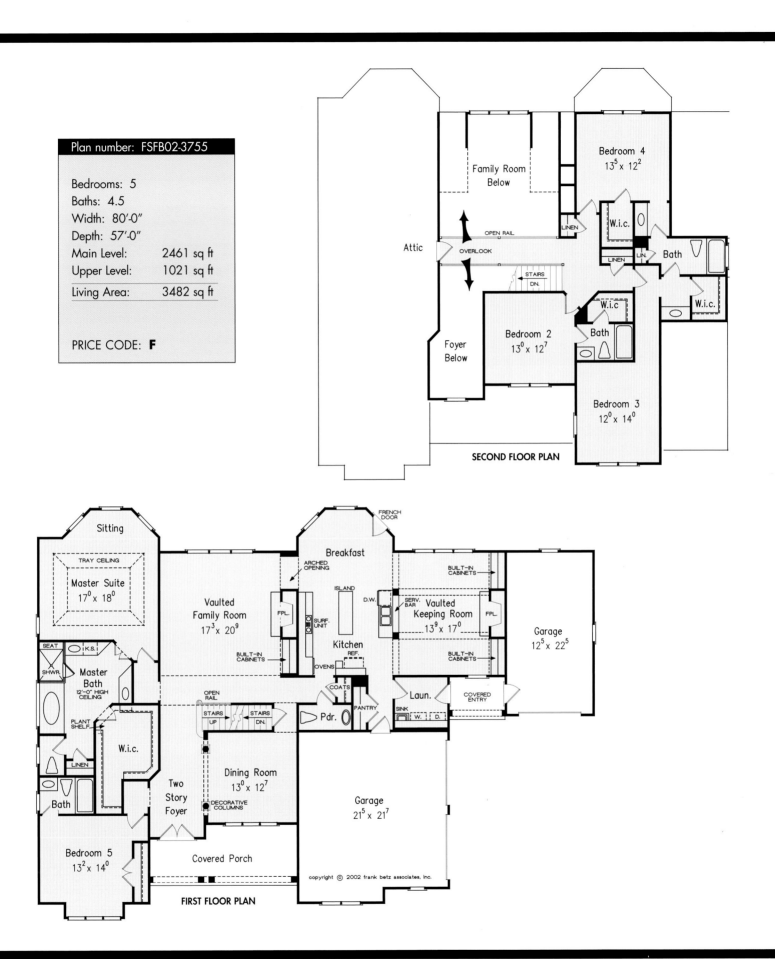

Plan number: FSFB02-3755

Bedrooms: 5
Baths: 4.5
Width: 80'-0"
Depth: 57'-0"
Main Level: 2461 sq ft
Upper Level: 1021 sq ft
Living Area: 3482 sq ft

PRICE CODE: **F**

SECOND FLOOR PLAN

Family Room Below

Attic

OPEN RAIL

OVERLOOK

STAIRS DN.

Foyer Below

Bedroom 2
13^0 x 12^7

W.i.c

Bath

LINEN

Bedroom 4
13^5 x 12^2

W.i.c

LINEN

LIN.

Bath

W.i.c.

Bedroom 3
12^0 x 14^0

FIRST FLOOR PLAN

Sitting

TRAY CEILING

Master Suite
17^0 x 18^0

SEAT

K.S.

SHWR.

Master Bath
12'-0" HIGH CEILING

PLANT SHELF

W.i.c.

LINEN

Bath

Bedroom 5
13^2 x 14^0

Two Story Foyer

OPEN RAIL

STAIRS UP

STAIRS DN.

DECORATIVE COLUMNS

Dining Room
13^0 x 12^7

Covered Porch

Vaulted Family Room
17^3 x 20^9

BUILT-IN CABINETS

FPL.

SURF. UNIT

OVENS

ARCHED OPENING

Breakfast

ISLAND

Kitchen

REF.

COATS

Pdr.

PANTRY

D.W.

SERV. BAR

Vaulted Keeping Room
13^9 x 17^0

BUILT-IN CABINETS

BUILT-IN CABINETS

FPL.

Laun.

SINK

W.

D.

COVERED ENTRY

Garage
12^5 x 22^5

Garage
21^5 x 21^7

FRENCH DOOR

copyright © 2002 frank betz associates, inc.

WOODCLIFFE

Casual elegance describes the Woodcliffe, with its timber-accented gables, a cupola, and weather vane atop the garage. Coffered ceilings create interesting dimension throughout the main level of this home. Art niches are designed at the top of the staircase providing innovative decorating opportunities. The master suite has a quiet sitting area with views to the backyard. A large family recreation room is incorporated into the upper level, providing flexible options like a media room or exercise area. An enormous optional bonus room on the upper level, suitable for a playroom or home office, gives the homeowner even more choices.

Rear Elevation

Plan number: FSFB02-3757

Bedrooms: 4
Baths: 3.5
Width: 68'-10"
Depth: 60'-0"
Main Level: 2225 sq ft
Upper Level: 1360 sq ft

Living Area: 3585 sq ft
Opt. Bonus Room 234 sq ft

PRICE CODE: **G**

SECOND FLOOR PLAN

W.i.c.

Bedroom 4
12⁰ x 13⁰

Family
Recreation Room
17³ x 20⁰

Optional
Bath

Bath

W.i.c.

STAIRS
UP

LINEN

NICHE   NICHE   NICHE

Attic

Bedroom 3
12⁷ x 13²

OPEN RAIL

OVERLOOK

LIN.

STAIRS
DN

PLANT SHELF

Bath

Bedroom 2
12³ x 14²

Foyer
Below

W.i.c.

Opt. Bonus
Room
11⁹ x 19⁰

FIRST FLOOR PLAN

Breakfast

COVERED
ENTRY

Sitting

COFFERED
CEILING

SERVING
BAR

FRENCH
DOOR

BUILT-IN
CAB.

TRAY CEILING

Vaulted
Keeping Room
11⁸ x 15⁶

FPL

D.W.

ISLAND

SURF.
UNIT

Family Room
17³ x 20⁰
10' - 9" COFFERED
CEILING

FPL.

Master Suite
15⁰ x 20³

Laundry

SINK

D.   W.

Kitchen

OVENS

BUILT-IN
CAB.

PKT. DOOR

LIN.

SHWR.

PANTRY

REF.

DECORATIVE
COLUMNS

Pdr.

K.S.

Vaulted
M. Bath

RADIUS
WINDOW

COATS

STAIRS
DN

OPEN RAIL

STAIRS
UP

Garage
22⁵ x 32⁵

DECORATIVE
COLUMNS

Dining Room
13⁰ x 14²

Two
Story
Foyer

Hers

His

FIXED LOUV.
SHUTTERS

Covered Porch

copyright © 2002 frank betz associates, inc.

© Frank Betz Associates, Inc.

ADDISON PLACE

DESIGN NOTES | A courtyard entry and dormered roofline create interesting dimension on the façade of the Addison Place. Subtle separation between the kitchen and keeping room allows for privacy, but still provides easy access from one to the other. Built-in cabinets allow homeowners to decorate with their own personal touch. Both bedrooms upstairs feature the luxury of a walk-in closet and share a divided bath. A large bonus area is available on the upper level that can be finished to suit the needs of the homeowner as a guest suite, media room or fourth bedroom.

SECOND FLOOR PLAN

Bedroom 3 13⁵ x 12⁰
Family Room Below
Bath
Bedroom 2 11² x 13²
Foyer Below
Opt. Bonus Room 12⁵ x 22¹⁰

FIRST FLOOR PLAN

Pantry
French Door
FPL
Breakfast
Ref.
Range / Island
Kitchen
DW.
Serving Bar
Tray Ceiling
Vaulted Family Room 16⁰ x 21⁶
Master Suite 13⁵ x 17⁰
Keeping Room 13⁵ x 15⁰
Open Rail
Stairs Up / Stairs Dn
Vaulted M.Bath
Radius Window
Built-In Cabinets
Pwdr.
FPL
Storage
Laund.
Dining Room 11⁰ x 13⁰
Two Story Foyer
Coats
W.i.c.
Covered Porch
Garage 20⁵ x 25⁹

copyright © 2003 frank betz associates, inc.

Plan number: FSFB02-3781

Bedrooms: 3
Baths: 2.5
Width: 51'-0"
Depth: 64'-0"

Main Level:	1816 sq ft
Upper Level:	684 sq ft
Living Area:	2500 sq ft
Opt. Bonus Room	422 sq ft

PRICE CODE: D

Rear Elevation

BLAKEFORD

DESIGN NOTES | The stunning two-story porch on this home is warm and inviting, while the rear covered porch is very practical. The openness of the breakfast area, kitchen, and keeping room adds sunlight and warmth. Fireplaces are located in the keeping room and the family room, allowing for formal as well as informal fireside gatherings.

SECOND FLOOR PLAN

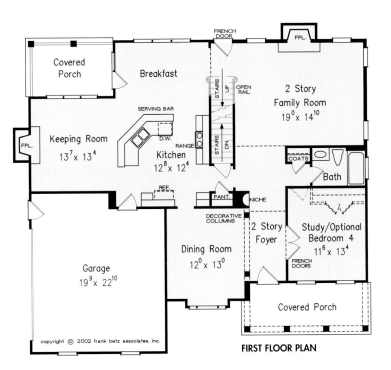

copyright © 2002 frank betz associates, inc.

FIRST FLOOR PLAN

Rear Elevation

Plan number: FSFB02-3753	
Bedrooms:	4
Baths:	4
Width:	52'-4"
Depth:	47'-4"
Main Level:	1444 sq ft
Upper Level:	1191 sq ft
Living Area:	2635 sq ft
Opt. Bonus Room	186 sq ft
PRICE CODE:	**E**

© Frank Betz Associates, Inc.

NORDSTROM

DESIGN NOTES | An age-old turret with eye-catching radius windows is the focal point of this not-so-traditional ranch design. Although the façade of the Nordstrom is quite traditional, today's latest and greatest design trends are waiting inside. A massive family room is especially unique with a coffered ceiling, built-in cabinets and backdrop of radius windows. The kitchen adjoins a vaulted keeping room with a fireplace – a comfortable place to relax for the evening. Everyone's needs are a bit different, so flexible spaces have been carefully incorporated. The formal living room can be easily converted into a sitting area for the master bedroom. Upstairs, an optional bedroom and bath make the perfect guest suite or home office.

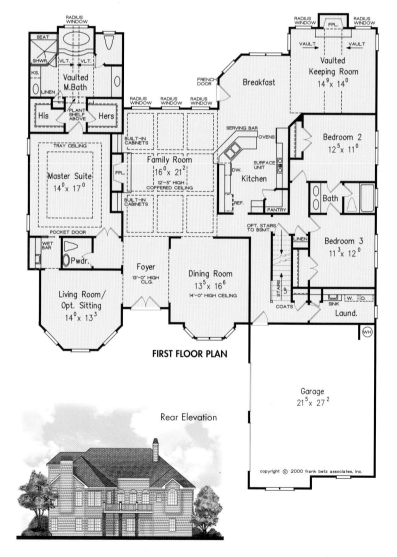

FIRST FLOOR PLAN

OPT. SECOND FLOOR PLAN

Rear Elevation

Plan number: FSFB02-3561
Bedrooms: 4
Baths: 3.5
Width: 60'-0"
Depth: 79'-4"
Main Level: 2713 sq ft
Living Area: 2713 sq ft
Opt. Second Floor 324 sq ft
PRICE CODE: **F**

© Frank Betz Associates, Inc.

CLEARBROOK

DESIGN NOTES | Stone accents charm the exterior of the Clearbrook design, giving it tons of character and curb appeal. But the real beauty is inside. Ingenious design and details make this home truly one of a kind! A dramatic keeping room with a unique octagonal shape adjoins the kitchen area. Coffered ceilings and built-in cabinetry make the family room interesting and original. The study easily converts into an additional bedroom, accommodating larger families. Even more space is available by adding the optional second floor. This space makes an ideal home office, playroom or bedroom.

FIRST FLOOR PLAN

Rear Elevation

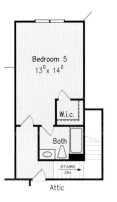

OPT. SECOND FLOOR PLAN

Plan number: FSFB02-3631	
Bedrooms: 5	
Baths: 4	
Width: 70'-0"	
Depth: 63'-0"	
Main Level:	2723 sq ft
Living Area:	2723 sq ft
Opt. Second Floor	375 sq ft
PRICE CODE: **E**	

© Frank Betz Associates, Inc.

GLENHAVEN

DESIGN NOTES | The Glenhaven's façade is original and eye-catching with its unique blend of finishing techniques. The inside is equally intriguing with a few special features that make it different from its counterparts. The kitchen overlooks a warm and casual keeping room. Transom windows allow plenty of natural light to pour into this area. Upstairs, bedroom two has a private bath, making it the perfect room for out-of-town guests. An optional bonus area is available on the upper level. Opting to finish it could result in a playroom, home office or fitness area.

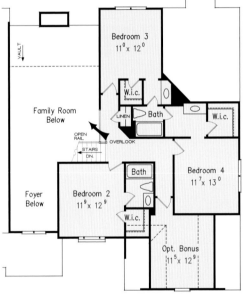

SECOND FLOOR PLAN

Bedroom 3
11⁰ x 12⁰

VAULT

Family Room Below

W.i.c.
LINEN
Bath
W.i.c.

OPEN RAIL
STAIRS DN.
OVERLOOK

Bath

Foyer Below

Bedroom 2
11⁹ x 12⁹

Bedroom 4
11⁷ x 13⁰

W.i.c.

Opt. Bonus
11⁵ x 12⁹

Plan number: **FSFB02-3613**	
Bedrooms: 4	
Baths: 3.5	
Width: 56'-0"	
Depth: 51'-4"	
Main Level:	1900 sq ft
Upper Level:	827 sq ft
Living Area:	2727 sq ft
Opt. Bonus Room	165 sq ft
PRICE CODE: **E**	

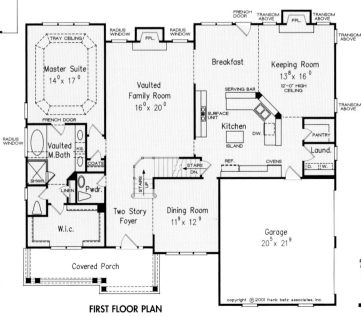

FIRST FLOOR PLAN

TRAY CEILING

Master Suite
14⁰ x 17⁰

RADIUS WINDOW
FPL
RADIUS WINDOW

FRENCH DOOR
TRANSOM ABOVE
FPL
TRANSOM ABOVE

Breakfast

Keeping Room
13⁸ x 16⁰
12'-0" HIGH CEILING

TRANSOM ABOVE

Vaulted Family Room
16⁰ x 20⁰

SERVING BAR

SURFACE UNIT

Kitchen
ISLAND
DW.

PANTRY
Laund.

TRANSOM ABOVE

FRENCH DOOR

RADIUS WINDOW

Vaulted M.Bath

KS.

COATS
SHWR.
LINEN
Pwdr.

STAIRS DN.
STAIRS UP

REF.
OVENS

D. W.

Two Story Foyer

Dining Room
11⁹ x 12⁹

Garage
20⁵ x 21⁹

W.i.c.

Covered Porch

copyright © 2001 frank betz associates, inc.

Rear Elevation

© Frank Betz Associates, Inc.

KEENELAND

DESIGN NOTES | Craftsman-style detailing gives the façade of the Keeneland the extra zest that many homeowners are in search of. Fieldstone and timber accents create a sense of warmth and welcome. Distinctive design elements can be found throughout this home. A cozy keeping room with a fireplace adjoins the kitchen and breakfast areas, creating a comfortable place to relax or entertain. Upstairs, a family center has been cleverly incorporated, wisely utilizing all of the available space on this floor. Many opt to use it as a multi-purpose family room, housing the computer, a television, toys or exercise equipment.

SECOND FLOOR PLAN

Family Center
16⁰ x 17⁹

Bedroom 4
12⁰ x 11⁸

Bedroom 3
11⁹ x 11⁶

STAIRS UP.

NICHE

STAIRS DN.

Foyer Below

Bath

W.i.c.

LIN.

Bedroom 2
12⁰ x 14³

PLANT SHELF

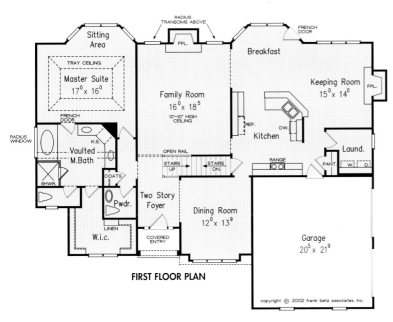

Sitting Area

TRAY CEILING

Master Suite
17⁰ x 16⁰

FRENCH DOOR

RADIUS WINDOW

Vaulted M.Bath

K.S.

COATS

SHWR

Pwdr.

LINEN

W.i.c.

Two Story Foyer

COVERED ENTRY

RADIUS TRANSOMS ABOVE

FPL.

Breakfast

FRENCH DOOR

Family Room
16⁰ x 18⁵
10'-10" HIGH CEILING

Kitchen

REF.

DW.

OPEN RAIL

STAIRS UP

STAIRS DN

RANGE

Keeping Room
15⁰ x 14⁰

FPL.

Laund.

PANT.

W.

D.

Dining Room
12⁰ x 13⁹

Garage
20⁵ x 21⁹

FIRST FLOOR PLAN

copyright © 2002 frank betz associates, inc.

Rear Elevation

Plan number: FSFB02-3758	
Bedrooms:	4
Baths:	2.5
Width:	60'-4"
Depth:	47'-6"
Main Level:	1780 sq ft
Upper Level:	1068 sq ft
Living Area:	2848 sq ft
PRICE CODE:	**E**

© Frank Betz Associates, Inc.

Bedroom 4
12⁶ x 11⁸

VAULT

Family Room
Below

Attic

Bath

LINEN

Bedroom 3
12⁷ x 12¹⁰

OVERLOOK

Bath

LIN.

STAIRS DN

W.i.c.

W.i.c.

Bedroom 2
12⁰ x 15⁴

Foyer
Below

OPEN RAIL

PLANT SHELF

SECOND FLOOR PLAN

BRADDOCK

DESIGN NOTES | Brick and siding give the Braddock a traditional flare on the outside, while today's most popular features are incorporated inside. A vaulted keeping room acts as a cozy extension of the kitchen and breakfast areas. Three secondary bedrooms, one with a bath, share the upper level of the home. Flexible space is designed with a fifth bedroom that can remain as such, or easily convert into a study.

FRENCH DOOR

Breakfast

FPL.

Sitting

FPL.

TRAY CEILING

Vaulted
Keeping Room
15⁸ x 12⁰

SERVING BAR

OVENS

Vaulted
Family Room
16⁰ x 19¹⁰

Master Suite
13⁰ x 19⁴

W.i.c.

Bath

SURFACE UNIT

DW.

Kitchen

FRENCH DOOR

COATS

SHWR.

DECORATIVE COLUMN

Bedroom 5
12⁰ x 10¹⁰

REF.

PANTRY

Laund.

D. W.

Two
Story
Foyer

STAIRS UP

STAIRS DN

KS.

Vaulted
M.Bath

LIN.

Dining Room
12⁰ x 12¹⁰

W.i.c.

Garage
21⁶ x 21⁹

Covered Porch

FIRST FLOOR PLAN

copyright © 2002 frank betz associates, inc.

Plan number: FSFB02-3725

Bedrooms: 5

Baths: 4

Width: 60'-10"

Depth: 55'-0"

Main Level: 1967 sq ft

Upper Level: 891 sq ft

Living Area: 2858 sq ft

PRICE CODE: **F**

Rear Elevation

© Frank Betz Associates, Inc.

COVINGTON RIDGE

DESIGN NOTES | Inventive and creative design elements set the Covington Ridge apart from other more common plans. The kitchen overlooks a warm and inviting keeping room, making an ideal location for laid-back time with family or friends. A work area serves as the command center of the home, giving homeowners designated space for a computer and household paperwork. The main floor bedroom can easily double as a home office. No details were overlooked in this smart design – decorative columns and built-in shelves are incorporated to add charm and character.

SECOND FLOOR PLAN

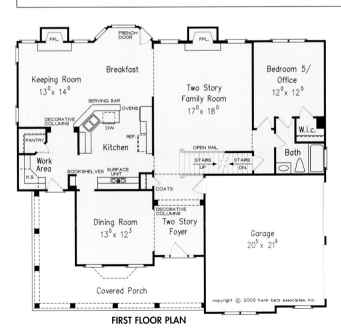

FIRST FLOOR PLAN

Rear Elevation

Plan number: **FSFB02-3792**

Bedrooms: 5
Baths: 4
Width: 53'-0"
Depth: 48'-0"
Main Level: 1558 sq ft
Upper Level: 1483 sq ft
Living Area: 3041 sq ft

PRICE CODE: **E**

© Frank Betz Associates, Inc.

McKENDREE PARK

DESIGN NOTES | The McKendree Park is a perfect combination of style and spaciousness. Generously sized rooms are accented with original detailing to create eye-appealing, open spaces. A dramatic coffered ceiling and bowed wall of windows give prominence to the already boastful grand room. Just off the kitchen, a comfortable keeping room offers an ideal location for casual family gatherings or entertaining. The master suite earns its name featuring a vaulted sitting area with tranquil backyard views. If extra space is what you need, an additional bonus area is available for a fourth bedroom or guest suite.

Rear Elevation

Plan number: FSFB02-3644

Bedrooms: 4

Baths: 3.5

Width: 89'-3"

Depth: 74'-3"

Main Level: 3168 sq ft

Living Area: 3168 sq ft

Opt. Second Floor 360 sq ft

PRICE CODE: **E**

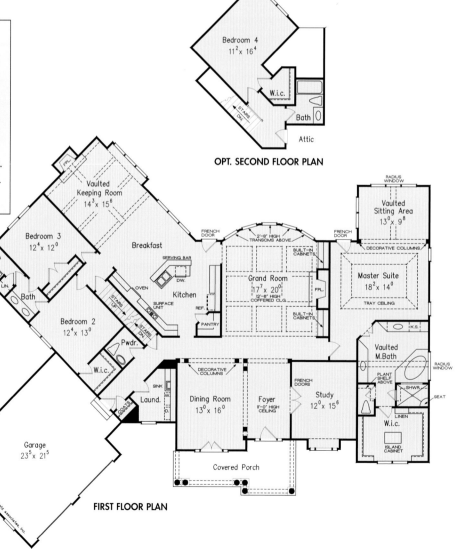

OPT. SECOND FLOOR PLAN

FIRST FLOOR PLAN

TO ORDER PLANS CALL TOLL FREE 888-717-3003

BENEDICT

DESIGN NOTES | The multi-faceted façade of the Benedict will pique the interest of passers-by. Multiple gables, a cheery dormer, and the classic combination of brick and siding make an impressive statement. Inside, an equally exciting floor plan awaits. The two-story foyer gives the perfect introduction to a vaulted grand room with built-in cabinetry and a wall of windows. Just beyond the kitchen is a vaulted keeping room with radius windows and a fireplace. The master suite includes a secluded lounging area that overlooks the backyard. A children's retreat is optional upstairs, making the ideal spot for toys, games and electronics.

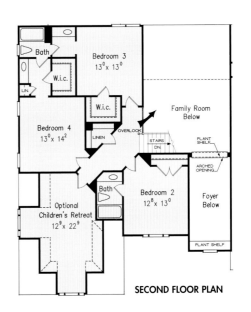

SECOND FLOOR PLAN

Bath
Bedroom 3
13⁰ x 13⁰
W.i.c.
LIN
W.i.c.
Bedroom 4
13⁰ x 14²
LINEN
OVERLOOK
Family Room Below
STAIRS DN
PLANT SHELF
ARCHED OPENING
Bath
Optional Children's Retreat
12⁹ x 22⁹
Bedroom 2
12⁸ x 13⁰
Foyer Below
PLANT SHELF

FIRST FLOOR PLAN

RADIUS WINDOW RADIUS WINDOW
FPL
Vaulted Keeping Room
14⁰ x 11⁰
FRENCH DOOR
FRENCH DOOR
Sitting
BUILT-IN CABINETS
TRAY CEILING
Breakfast
SERVING BAR
DW.
SURFACE UNIT
Kitchen
OVENS
Vaulted Grand Room
17⁰ x 20²
FPL
Master Suite
15² x 21⁰
BUILT-IN CABINETS
DESK
SINK
Laund.
D.   W.
REF.
PANTRY
COATS
STAIRS DN.
STAIRS UP
OPEN RAIL
DECORATIVE COLUMNS
FRENCH DOOR
M.Bath
12'-0" HIGH CEILING
Pwdr.
SHWR.
KS.
PLANT SHELF ABOVE
RADIUS WINDOW
Garage
20⁵ x 30⁰
Dining Room
13⁸ x 15²
Two Story Foyer
His
Hers
NICHE
PLANT SHELF ABOVE
LINEN
Living Room/Study
12⁵ x 14⁶
COVERED ENTRY

copyright © 2002 frank betz associates, inc.

Rear Elevation

Plan number: FSFB02-3768	
Bedrooms:	4
Baths:	3.5
Width:	60'-0"
Depth:	64'-4"
Main Level:	2355 sq ft
Upper Level:	946 sq ft
Living Area:	3301 sq ft
Opt. Bonus Room	275 sq ft
PRICE CODE:	**G**

© Frank Betz Associates, Inc.

CEDAR CREEK

DESIGN NOTES | One look and it's easy to see that inventive design and thoughtful attention to detail went into designing the Cedar Creek. A warm and cozy keeping room adjoins the kitchen area – perfect for casual family time and for hosting parties. Coffered ceilings, radius windows and built-in cabinetry come together to make the family room a unique gathering spot. Finishing the available optional space creates the perfect guest suite or home office, private from the rest of the home. A tranquil sitting area is incorporated into the master suite, perfect for a comfy chair and ottoman.

OPT. SECOND FLOOR PLAN

Bedroom 5
15¹⁰ x 12⁰

Plan number: FSFB02-3640

Bedrooms: 5

Baths: 4.5

Width: 70'-7"

Depth: 81'-10"

Main Level: 3418 sq ft

Living Area: 3418 sq ft

Opt. Second Floor 388 sq ft

PRICE CODE: **F**

FIRST FLOOR PLAN

Master Suite 14⁰ x 20⁹

Sitting

Family Room 17⁸ x 20⁰

Breakfast

Keeping Room 16² x 16⁰

Bedroom 2 13⁰ x 12⁰

Bedroom 3 13⁰ x 12⁰

Bedroom 4 13⁰ x 12⁴

Kitchen

Laund.

Dining Room 13³ x 14⁵

Foyer 12'-6" HIGH CEILING

Vaulted Study 13⁰ x 14⁰

Garage 21⁵ x 25⁹

copyright © 2001 frank betz associates, inc.

Rear Elevation

TO ORDER PLANS CALL TOLL FREE 888-717-3003

BELMEADE MANOR

DESIGN NOTES | The unique layout of the main floor is surpassed only by the floor above. A generous master suite is equipped with its own fireplace, walk-in closet, and spacious bathroom. On the main level, the cozy keeping room is adorned with its own fireplace, which adds more ambience to the breakfast room and kitchen. Built-in desks, cabinets, and pantries are nice amenities in this home.

SECOND FLOOR PLAN

FIRST FLOOR PLAN

Rear Elevation

Plan number: FSFB02-3762

Bedrooms: 5

Baths: 4

Width: 68'-7"

Depth: 62'-8"

Main Level: 1773 sq ft

Upper Level: 1676 sq ft

Living Area: 3449 sq ft

PRICE CODE: **F**

FLANAGAN

DESIGN NOTES | If your home is your castle, then the Flanagan is the design for you. A stunning stone turret gives this plan eye-catching curb appeal. More great surprises await you inside. A vaulted keeping room – accentuated by decorative columns – adjoins the kitchen area providing a warm and comfortable spot to spend casual time with family and friends. The master suite earns its name featuring a uniquely shaped sitting area; a relaxing spot to retire at the end of the day. A main floor bedroom can be easily converted into a den or home office.

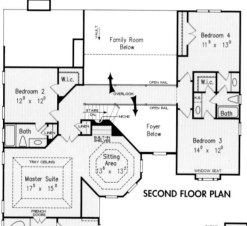

SECOND FLOOR PLAN

FIRST FLOOR PLAN

copyright © 1997 frank betz associates, inc.

Rear Elevation

Plan number: FSFB02-1058

Bedrooms: 5

Baths: 4.5

Width: 54'-0"

Depth: 78'-4"

Main Level: 2060 sq ft

Upper Level: 1817 sq ft

Living Area: 3877 sq ft

PRICE CODE: **G**

TO ORDER PLANS CALL TOLL FREE 888-717-3003

BROOKSHIRE MANOR

DESIGN NOTES | Class, style, tradition and every creature comfort imaginable – the Brookshire Manor grants every wish! Relax and unwind by the fire in the cozy hearth room adjoining the kitchen. The master suite earns its name featuring a personal lounging room with a fireplace, a lavish master bath with private dressing area, and direct access to the exercise room. A covered side entrance, butler's pantry and art niches are all added extras that make this home special. A covered wraparound porch and its gambrel roof over the garage make the façade welcoming.

SECOND FLOOR PLAN

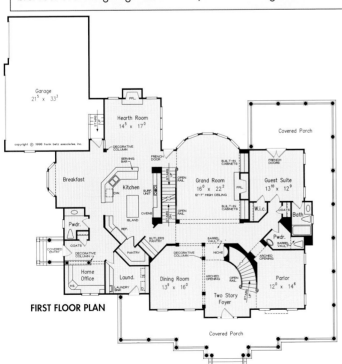

FIRST FLOOR PLAN

Rear Elevation

Plan number: FSFB02-1184

Bedrooms: 5

Baths: 5 full, 2 half

Width: 85'-0"

Depth: 85'-6"

Main Level: 2732 sq ft

Upper Level: 2734 sq ft

Living Area: 5466 sq ft

PRICE CODE: **G**

HOME
OFFICES

n the 21st-Century, every well-equipped home must have a home office, in the same way that older homes required a parlor or library. The office is essential as a planning center for the household, with a connection to the rest of the home. Links to the public and private areas of the design dictate that the office space serves as both a secluded conservatory and a flexible introduction to the rest of the home. With a textured palette of architectural amenities, such as built-in cabinetry and massive hearths, the space takes on a different character when converted to a study or a den. With ample space for computers and business furnishings, the home office must also be an inviting space in which to meet and greet clients. Placed near the front or side entry in Greenwich [page 72], the room adjoins a powder bath and can include a privacy set of French doors. ▓

Left | Four light transom windows allow sunshine into this lofty home office. Wall space below the windows provide for a custom memo board.

© Frank Betz Associates, Inc.

SEYMOUR

Style and sensibility meet to create the Seymour, a design that is as practical as it is beautiful. Fieldstone, copper accents and a courtyard entry distinguish this home from the others on the block. The main floor consists of the common living areas, master suite and one secondary bedroom that can easily serve as the home office. Upstairs, two bedrooms share a bath. Optional bonus space is also available on the second floor, leaving homeowners with choices on how to finish it. This space is ideal for a playroom or fitness area.

Rear Elevation

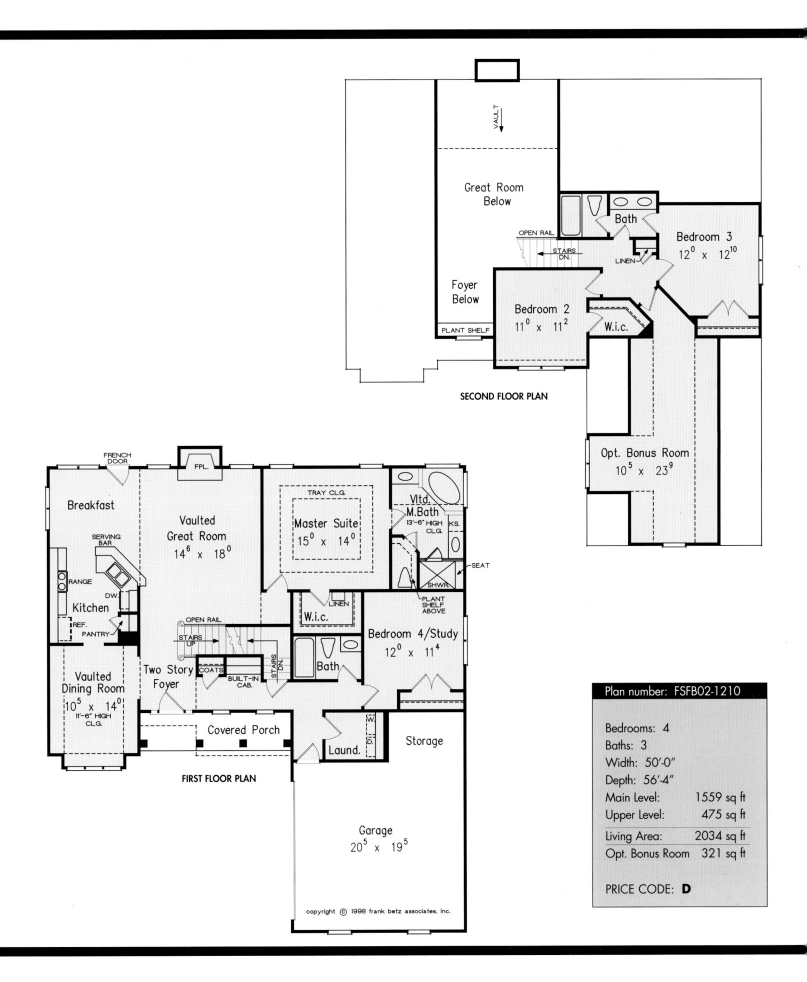

SECOND FLOOR PLAN

Great Room Below

VAULT

Bath

Bedroom 3
12^0 x 12^{10}

OPEN RAIL

STAIRS DN.

LINEN

Foyer Below

Bedroom 2
11^0 x 11^2

W.i.c.

PLANT SHELF

Opt. Bonus Room
10^5 x 23^9

FRENCH DOOR

FPL.

Breakfast

SERVING BAR

RANGE

DW.

Kitchen

REF.

PANTRY

Vaulted Great Room
14^6 x 18^0

TRAY CLG.

Master Suite
15^0 x 14^0

Vltd. M.Bath
13'-6" HIGH CLG.

KS.

SEAT

SHWR.

PLANT SHELF ABOVE

W.i.c.

LINEN

OPEN RAIL

STAIRS UP

STAIRS DN.

Bath

Bedroom 4/Study
12^0 x 11^4

Vaulted Dining Room
10^5 x 14^0
11'-6" HIGH CLG.

Two Story Foyer

COATS

BUILT-IN CAB.

Covered Porch

Laund.

W. D.

Storage

Garage
20^5 x 19^5

FIRST FLOOR PLAN

copyright © 1998 frank betz associates, inc.

Plan number: FSFB02-1210

Bedrooms: 4
Baths: 3
Width: 50'-0"
Depth: 56'-4"
Main Level: 1559 sq ft
Upper Level: 475 sq ft
Living Area: 2034 sq ft
Opt. Bonus Room   321 sq ft

PRICE CODE: **D**

© Frank Betz Associates, Inc.

COLONNADE

Many homeowners today want function with flexibility. The Colonnade was created to provide both of these elements. The family room, kitchen and breakfast area connect to create the home's center point. The size and location of the main floor bedroom also make it a perfect home office or den. Optional bonus space on the upper level of this home gives homeowners the opportunity to add additional living space to their home. The generous dimensions of this room leave many choices for how the space can be used. One upstairs bedroom has a vaulted ceiling adding unique dimension to the room.

Rear Elevation

Family Room
Below

VAULT

Bath

Bedroom 3
12^8 x 13^0

W.i.c.

STAIRS
DN.

OPEN
RAIL

PLANT
SHELF

Foyer
Below

Vaulted
Bedroom 2
11^2 x 11^8

LINEN

W.i.c.

Opt. Bonus
11^5 x 19^4

SECOND FLOOR PLAN

TRAY CEILING

FPL.

FRENCH
DOOR

Breakfast

Bedroom 4
11^0 x 10^0

Master Suite
13^0 x 17^0

Vaulted
Family Room
16^0 x 18^0

SERVING BAR

PANT.

REF.

RANGE

Kitchen

REF.

Bath

W. D.

FRENCH DOOR

RADIUS
WINDOW

Vaulted
M.Bath

COATS

STAIRS
DN.

Laund.

SHWR.

LINEN

PLANT
SHELF
ABOVE

W.i.c.

STAIRS
UP

Two
Story
Foyer

Dining Room
11^2 x 12^2

Garage
19^5 x 22^8

Covered Porch

FIRST FLOOR PLAN

copyright © 2002 frank betz associates, inc.

Plan number: FSFB02-3699

Bedrooms: 4
Baths: 3
Width: 53'-0"
Depth: 47'-6"
Main Level: 1589 sq ft
Upper Level: 549 sq ft

Living Area: 2138 sq ft
Opt. Bonus Room 248 sq ft

PRICE CODE: **E**

© Frank Betz Associates, Inc.

STONINGTON

T wo-story spaces in the foyer and family room make a grand impression. A walk-in pantry adds convenience to the kitchen. The secondary bedroom on the main level is just steps from the master suite and is a convenient spot for a home office or nursery. Upstairs, each secondary bedroom has a walk-in closet.

Rear Elevation

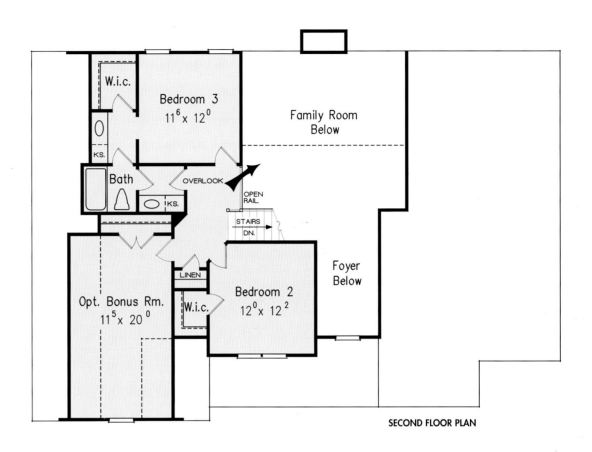

W.i.c.

Bedroom 3
11⁶ x 12⁰

Family Room Below

KS.

Bath OVERLOOK

OPEN RAIL

Foyer Below

KS.

STAIRS DN.

LINEN

Opt. Bonus Rm.
11⁵ x 20⁰

W.i.c.

Bedroom 2
12⁰ x 12²

SECOND FLOOR PLAN

FRENCH DOOR

FPL.

Breakfast

TRAY CEILING

RANGE   DW.

Kitchen

REF.

Master Suite
17⁰ x 13⁶

PANTRY

Laund.   COATS

D. W

Storage

Vaulted Family Room
18⁸ x 17⁰

Vaulted M.Bath

KS.

PLANT SHELF ABOVE

STAIRS DN.   STAIRS UP

Bath

SHWR.

Garage
19⁵ x 22⁸

Dining Room
12⁰ x 12²

Two Story Foyer

Vaulted Bedroom 4/ Hm. Office
11⁰ x 12⁷

W.i.c.

LINEN

copyright © 2000 frank betz associates, inc.

Covered Porch

FIRST FLOOR PLAN

Plan number: FSFB02-3567

Bedrooms: 4
Baths: 3
Width: 60'-0"
Depth: 42'-10"
Main Level: 1714 sq ft
Upper Level: 537 sq ft
Living Area: 2251 sq ft
Opt. Bonus Room 260 sq ft

PRICE CODE: **D**

© Frank Betz Associates, Inc.

DEFOORS MILL

Tradition is appreciated in the thoughtful design of Defoors Mill. A covered porch is situated on the front of the home and leads to a charming and practical floor plan. The master suite encompasses an entire wing of the home for comfort and privacy. Special details in this home include a handy island in the kitchen, a coat closet just off the garage, and optional bonus space upstairs.

Rear Elevation

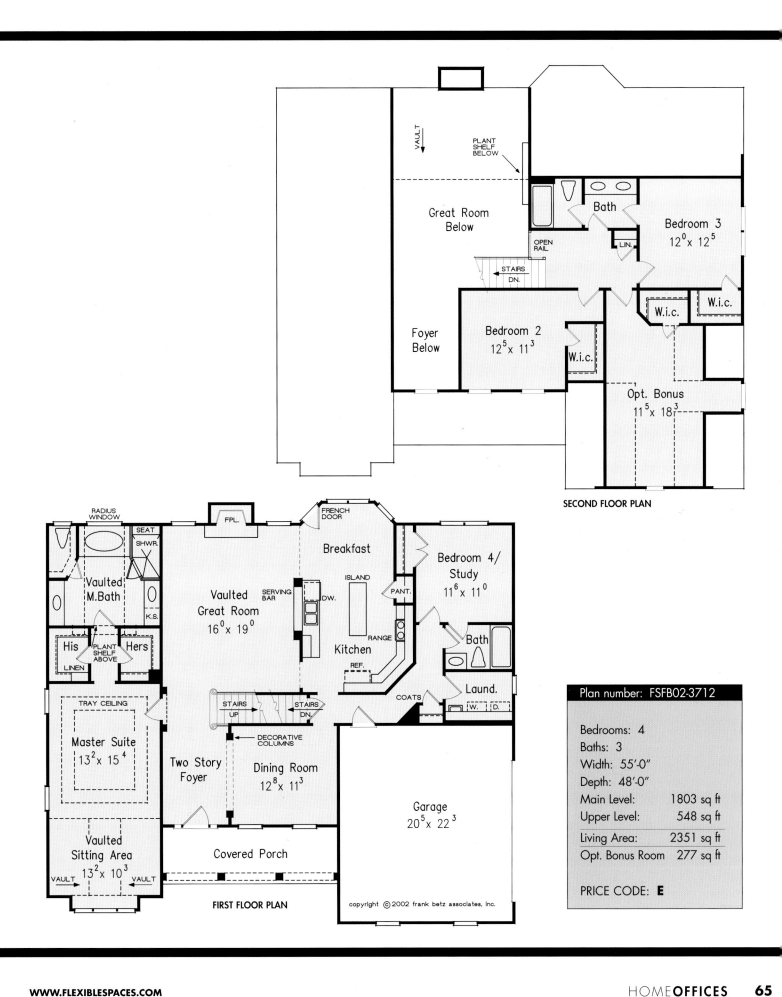

VAULT

PLANT SHELF BELOW

Great Room Below

Bath

Bedroom 3
12⁰ x 12⁵

OPEN RAIL

LIN.

STAIRS DN.

Foyer Below

Bedroom 2
12⁵ x 11³

W.i.c.

W.i.c.

W.i.c.

Opt. Bonus
11⁵ x 18³

SECOND FLOOR PLAN

RADIUS WINDOW

SEAT

SHWR.

FPL

FRENCH DOOR

Breakfast

Bedroom 4/ Study
11⁶ x 11⁰

Vaulted M.Bath

K.S.

His

PLANT SHELF ABOVE

Hers

LINEN

Vaulted Great Room
16⁰ x 19⁰

SERVING BAR

DW.

ISLAND

PANT.

RANGE

REF.

Kitchen

Bath

TRAY CEILING

STAIRS UP

STAIRS DN.

COATS

Laund.

W. D.

Master Suite
13² x 15⁴

DECORATIVE COLUMNS

Two Story Foyer

Dining Room
12⁸ x 11³

Garage
20⁵ x 22³

Vaulted Sitting Area
13² x 10³

VAULT

VAULT

Covered Porch

FIRST FLOOR PLAN

copyright © 2002 frank betz associates, inc.

Plan number: FSFB02-3712

Bedrooms: 4
Baths: 3
Width: 55'-0"
Depth: 48'-0"
Main Level: 1803 sq ft
Upper Level: 548 sq ft

Living Area: 2351 sq ft
Opt. Bonus Room   277 sq ft

PRICE CODE: **E**

CULPEPPER

Sand-hued clapboard siding enriches the brick gables of this time-honored design. A classic colonnade provides a pleasing perimeter for the entry porch, which is capped by a standing-seam roof. Inside, the two-story foyer opens to a formal dining room and to a vaulted family room, with a fireplace and views to the backyard. Graceful archways and a pass-through link the central living space with the kitchen and breakfast bay, while a French door grants access to the outdoors. The master suite provides a sitting bay and a vaulted bath. A wrapping gallery hall conveniently connects a utility area with guest quarters.

Rear Elevation

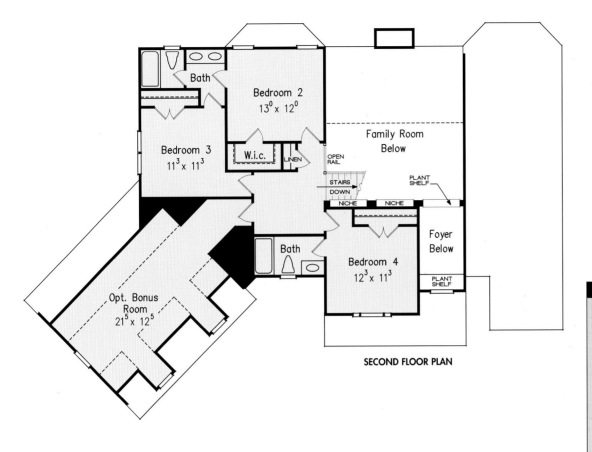

SECOND FLOOR PLAN

- Bath
- Bedroom 2 — 13⁰ x 12⁰
- Bedroom 3 — 11³ x 11³
- W.i.c.
- LINEN
- OPEN RAIL
- STAIRS DOWN
- NICHE   NICHE
- Family Room Below
- PLANT SHELF
- Foyer Below
- Bath
- Bedroom 4 — 12³ x 11³
- PLANT SHELF
- Opt. Bonus Room — 21⁵ x 12⁵

Plan number: FSFB02-3765	
Bedrooms:	5
Baths:	4
Width:	72'-7"
Depth:	51'-5"
Main Level:	1809 sq ft
Upper Level:	785 sq ft
Living Area:	2594 sq ft
Opt. Bonus Room	353 sq ft

PRICE CODE: **D**

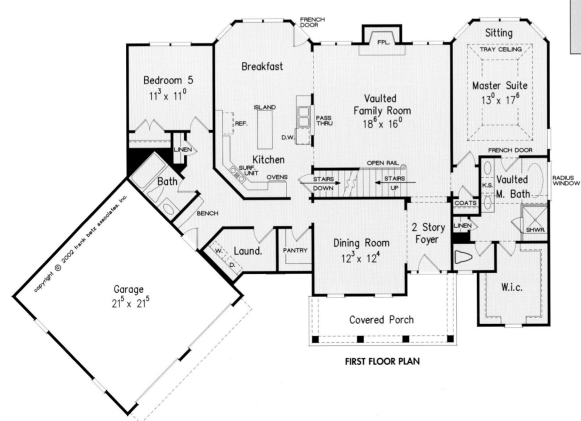

FIRST FLOOR PLAN

- FRENCH DOOR
- Breakfast
- FPL.
- Sitting
- TRAY CEILING
- Bedroom 5 — 11³ x 11⁰
- ISLAND
- PASS THRU
- D.W.
- REF.
- Master Suite — 13⁰ x 17⁶
- LINEN
- Kitchen
- Vaulted Family Room — 18⁶ x 16⁰
- SURF. UNIT
- OVENS
- Bath
- OPEN RAIL
- STAIRS DOWN   STAIRS UP
- FRENCH DOOR
- K.S.
- Vaulted M. Bath
- RADIUS WINDOW
- BENCH
- COATS
- 2 Story Foyer
- LINEN
- SHWR.
- W.   Laund.   PANTRY
- D.
- Dining Room — 12³ x 12⁴
- W.i.c.
- copyright © 2002 frank betz associates, inc.
- Garage — 21⁵ x 21⁵
- Covered Porch

© Frank Betz Associates, Inc.

MICHELLE

Arched and bay windows complement vaulted and tray ceilings to make this home bright and cheery. The family room fireplace is on an interior wall to make room for windows on the rear wall. Built-in bookshelves flanking the fireplace make wonderful areas for storage or display. We included a vaulted ceiling and windows when designing the breakfast area too. The master suite has a tray ceiling and an arched window. A main-level secondary bedroom makes an ideal guest suite or home office.

Rear Elevation

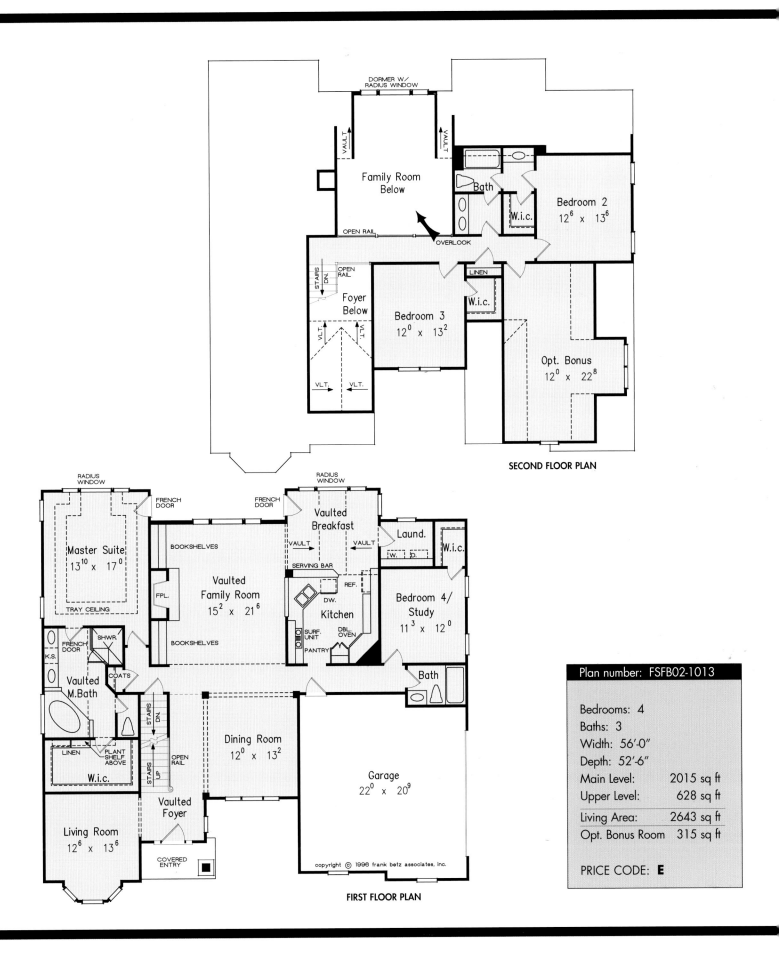

DORMER W/ RADIUS WINDOW

VAULT VAULT

Family Room Below

Bath

W.i.c.

Bedroom 2
12⁶ x 13⁶

OPEN RAIL

OVERLOOK

STAIRS DN.

OPEN RAIL

LINEN

Foyer Below

Bedroom 3
12⁰ x 13²

W.i.c.

VLT. VLT.

VLT. VLT.

Opt. Bonus
12⁰ x 22⁸

SECOND FLOOR PLAN

RADIUS WINDOW

FRENCH DOOR

FRENCH DOOR

RADIUS WINDOW

Vaulted Breakfast

Laund.

W.i.c.

Master Suite
13¹⁰ x 17⁰

BOOKSHELVES

VAULT VAULT

w. p.

TRAY CEILING

FPL.

Vaulted Family Room
15² x 21⁶

SERVING BAR

REF.

Bedroom 4/ Study
11³ x 12⁰

SHWR.

BOOKSHELVES

Kitchen

DW.

DBL. OVEN

K.S.

French Door

COATS

SURF. UNIT

PANTRY

Vaulted M.Bath

LINEN

PLANT SHELF ABOVE

W.i.c.

STAIRS DN.

STAIRS UP

OPEN RAIL

Dining Room
12⁰ x 13²

Bath

Living Room
12⁶ x 13⁶

Vaulted Foyer

Garage
22⁰ x 20⁹

COVERED ENTRY

copyright © 1996 frank betz associates, inc.

FIRST FLOOR PLAN

Plan number: FSFB02-1013	
Bedrooms:	4
Baths:	3
Width:	56'-0"
Depth:	52'-6"
Main Level:	2015 sq ft
Upper Level:	628 sq ft
Living Area:	2643 sq ft
Opt. Bonus Room	315 sq ft

PRICE CODE: **E**

© Frank Betz Associates, Inc.

NEYLAND

Neighborhoods of new and old welcome a design like the Neyland. Warm brick and friendly dormers create a well-established, time-tested façade. The design inside is fresh and innovative, featuring some of today's most popular trends. The master suite houses its own private sitting area, giving the homeowner a place to retreat to after a busy day. A fifth bedroom on the main level makes a great guest room or can be easily changed to a den. The kitchen has everything the busy family or entertainer could need, complete with an island, double ovens, and a walk-in pantry.

Rear Elevation

TO ORDER PLANS CALL TOLL FREE 888-717-3003

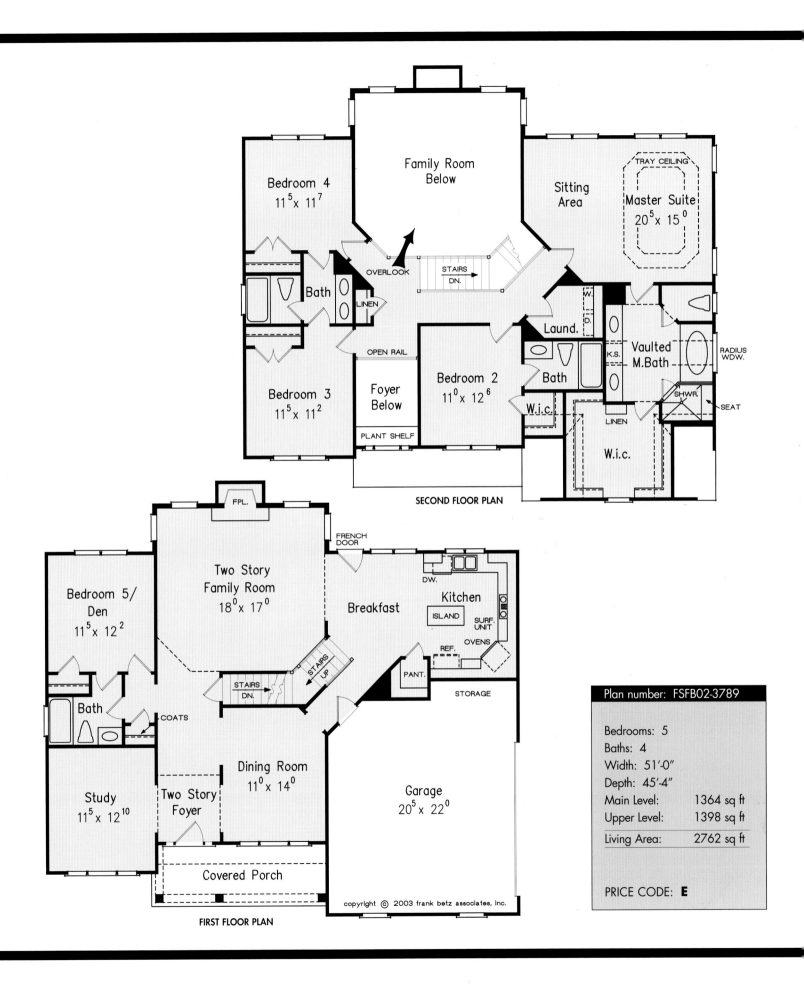

Family Room Below

Bedroom 4
11^5 x 11^7

Sitting Area

TRAY CEILING

Master Suite
20^5 x 15^0

Bath

LINEN

OVERLOOK

STAIRS DN.

W. D.

Laund.

Vaulted M.Bath

RADIUS WDW.

OPEN RAIL

Bedroom 3
11^5 x 11^2

Foyer Below

Bedroom 2
11^0 x 12^6

Bath

W.i.c.

K.S.

LINEN

SHWR.

SEAT

PLANT SHELF

W.i.c.

SECOND FLOOR PLAN

FPL.

FRENCH DOOR

Two Story Family Room
18^0 x 17^0

Breakfast

Kitchen

DW.

ISLAND

SURF. UNIT

OVENS

REF.

Bedroom 5/ Den
11^5 x 12^2

STAIRS UP

STAIRS DN.

PANT.

STORAGE

Bath

COATS

Study
11^5 x 12^{10}

Two Story Foyer

Dining Room
11^0 x 14^0

Garage
20^5 x 22^0

Covered Porch

copyright © 2003 frank betz associates, inc.

FIRST FLOOR PLAN

Plan number: FSFB02-3789

Bedrooms: 5
Baths: 4
Width: 51'-0"
Depth: 45'-4"
Main Level: 1364 sq ft
Upper Level: 1398 sq ft
Living Area: 2762 sq ft

PRICE CODE: **E**

© Frank Betz Associates, Inc.

GREENWICH

This eye-catching façade commands attention. A massive archway over the double-door entrance is a dramatic starting point. The design inside is equally as exciting. A bright two-story family room sets the stage for a home that's upscale everywhere you look. The kitchen surrounds a large island with serving bar, big enough to use for casual dining. A bedroom on the main floor can be used as such or converted into a study or den. The master suite houses its own private sitting area, accented with an arched opening. Bedroom three is particularly interesting with a unique, partially vaulted ceiling and a window seat.

Rear Elevation

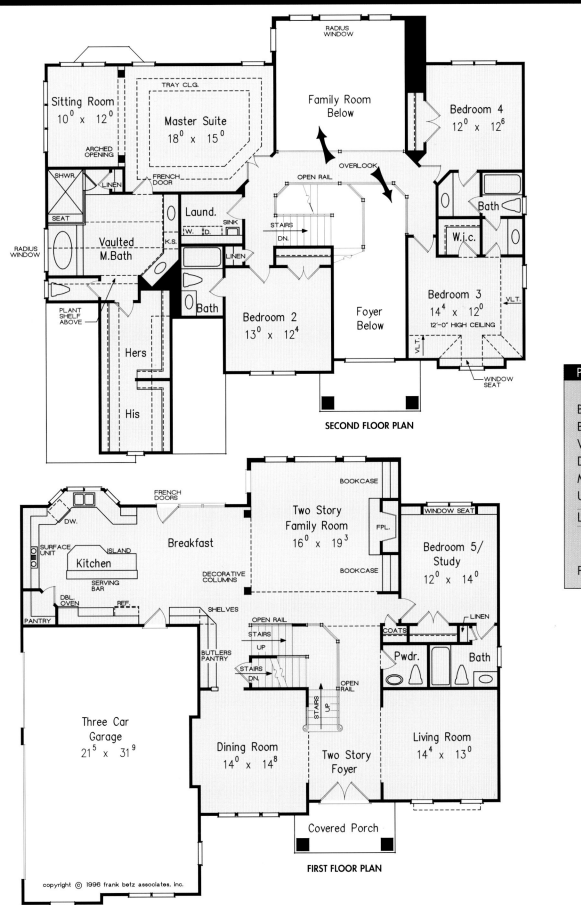

SECOND FLOOR PLAN

Sitting Room
10⁰ x 12⁰

TRAY CLG.

Master Suite
18⁰ x 15⁰

Family Room
Below

RADIUS WINDOW

Bedroom 4
12⁰ x 12⁶

ARCHED OPENING

SHWR.

SEAT

LINEN

FRENCH DOOR

OVERLOOK

OPEN RAIL

Bath

RADIUS WINDOW

Vaulted M.Bath

K.S.

Laund.

W. D.

SINK

STAIRS DN.

LINEN

W.i.c.

PLANT SHELF ABOVE

Hers

Bath

Bedroom 2
13⁰ x 12⁴

Foyer Below

Bedroom 3
14⁴ x 12⁰
12'-0" HIGH CEILING

VLT.

His

VLT.

WINDOW SEAT

FIRST FLOOR PLAN

FRENCH DOORS

BOOKCASE

DW.

SURFACE UNIT

ISLAND

Kitchen

SERVING BAR

DECORATIVE COLUMNS

Two Story Family Room
16⁰ x 19³

FPL.

Breakfast

BOOKCASE

WINDOW SEAT

Bedroom 5/ Study
12⁰ x 14⁰

DBL. OVEN

REF.

SHELVES

PANTRY

BUTLERS PANTRY

OPEN RAIL

STAIRS UP

STAIRS DN.

OPEN RAIL

COATS

LINEN

Pwdr.

Bath

Three Car Garage
21⁵ x 31⁹

STAIRS UP

Dining Room
14⁰ x 14⁸

Two Story Foyer

Living Room
14⁴ x 13⁰

Covered Porch

Plan number: FSFB02-1003	
Bedrooms: 5	
Baths: 4.5	
Width: 59'-0"	
Depth: 53'-0"	
Main Level:	1786 sq ft
Upper Level:	1739 sq ft
Living Area:	3525 sq ft

PRICE CODE: **G**

© Frank Betz Associates, Inc.

PFEIFFER

DESIGN NOTES | The flexible spaces in this design give homeowners options on how they want their finished home to function. The master suite has an optional sitting area available that gives homeowners a restful retreat or can easily house a desk or treadmill. A key feature in this design is its towering grand room. A complete two stories high, this room creates a dramatic center of the home. The laundry room is located on the upper level to accommodate the primary bedrooms.

LINEN
W.i.c.
VAULT
Vaulted M.Bath
SHWR

Bedroom 3
11^3 x 10^4

Grand Room Below

LINEN
Bath
OPEN RAIL

OVERLOOK
OPEN RAIL

TRAY CEILING

Master Suite
17^2 x 13^0

STAIRS DN.

Bedroom 2
11^3 x 11^6

W D Laund.

Opt. Sitting
9^5 x 11^3

SECOND FLOOR PLAN

Plan number: FSFB02-3553
Bedrooms: 4
Baths: 3
Width: 47'-0"
Depth: 37'-4"
Main Level: 990 sq ft
Upper Level: 912 sq ft
Living Area: 1902 sq ft
Opt. Bonus Room 116 sq ft
PRICE CODE: C

Bedroom 4/ Home Office
10^0 x 11^5

Bath
Breakfast
PANTRY
FRENCH DOOR
FPL.

COATS
DW.
RANGE
Kitchen
REF.

Two Story Grand Room
15^0 x 17^0

OPEN RAIL

Garage
19^5 x 22^8

STAIRS DN.

Dining Room
11^3 x 10^0

Foyer

STAIRS UP

Covered Porch

copyright © 2000 frank betz associates, inc.

FIRST FLOOR PLAN

Rear Elevation

© Frank Betz Associates, Inc.

TUSCANY

DESIGN NOTES | Thoughtful and innovative, the Tuscany incorporates many features often only found in larger homes. A towering two-story family room is the prominent feature on the main level of the home. A large island and a built-in message center are incorporated into the kitchen area, making day-to-day living convenient and organized. The dining room and kitchen are connected by a butler's pantry. The main floor bedroom is easily converted into a home office. Bonus space is available on the second floor, creating the perfect space for an additional bedroom, children's retreat or home gym.

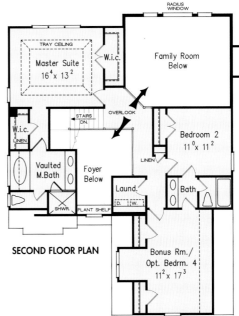

SECOND FLOOR PLAN

FIRST FLOOR PLAN

copyright © 2001 frank betz associates, inc.

Rear Elevation

Plan number:	FSFB02-3630
Bedrooms:	4
Baths:	3
Width:	41'-4"
Depth:	50'-0"
Main Level:	1187 sq ft
Upper Level:	801 sq ft
Living Area:	1988 sq ft
Opt. Bonus Room	258 sq ft
PRICE CODE:	**C**

© Frank Betz Associates, Inc.

STRATFORD PLACE

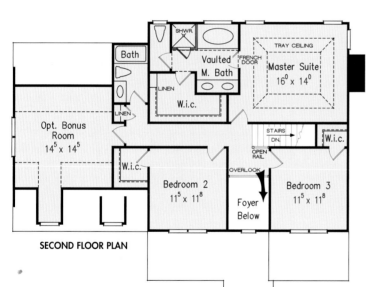

SECOND FLOOR PLAN

- Bath
- SHWR.
- Vaulted M. Bath
- FRENCH DOOR
- TRAY CEILING
- Master Suite 16⁰ x 14⁰
- LINEN
- LINEN
- W.i.c.
- Opt. Bonus Room 14⁵ x 14⁵
- STAIRS DN.
- W.i.c.
- OPEN RAIL
- W.i.c.
- OVERLOOK
- Bedroom 2 11⁵ x 11⁸
- Bedroom 3 11⁵ x 11⁸
- Foyer Below

DESIGN NOTES | Simple and uncomplicated, the Stratford Place has an understated elegance that can be found in the quaintest neighborhoods of today and yesterday. The breakfast and family rooms share common space with the kitchen, catering to casual and easy interaction from one area to the next. The main floor bedroom – with direct access to a bath – makes the perfect guest suite or can be easily used as a home office. An optional bonus room upstairs gives the growing family some extra space – ideal for a children's retreat or family recreation area. Bedrooms two and three share a bath and feature walk-in closets.

FIRST FLOOR PLAN

- Stor.
- D. W.
- Laun.
- PANTRY
- Breakfast
- FRENCH DOOR
- Family Room 18⁰ x 14⁰
- FPL.
- KNEEWALL
- RANGE
- D.W.
- Kitchen
- REF.
- Garage 19⁹ x 20²
- OPEN RAIL
- STAIRS DN.
- STAIRS UP
- COATS
- Bath
- Dining Room 11⁵ x 11⁰
- Two Story Foyer
- copyright © 2002 frank betz associates, inc.
- Bedroom 4 11⁵ x 11⁰
- Covered Porch

Rear Elevation

Plan number: FSFB02-3748	
Bedrooms:	4
Baths:	3
Width:	52'-4"
Depth:	38'-6"
Main Level:	1063 sq ft
Upper Level:	929 sq ft
Living Area:	1992 sq ft
Opt. Bonus Room	246 sq ft
PRICE CODE:	C

LESHAYE

DESIGN NOTES | Buttery yellow lap siding sets off this casual façade, combining a charming country spirit with the classic colonial lines of the American vernacular. Winding stairs frame the two-story foyer and define an open hall that leads to the family room. Decorative columns and a fireplace framed by two sets of windows set a refined theme for this central living space. An island counter anchors the kitchen, which shares a wall of glass and outdoor access with the breakfast area. To the front of the plan, a home office with ample wardrobe space and a nearby bath, easily converts to guest quarters.

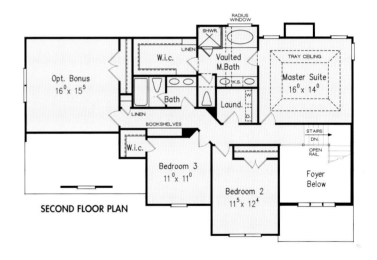

SECOND FLOOR PLAN

- Opt. Bonus 16⁰ x 15⁵
- RADIUS WINDOW
- SHWR.
- LINEN
- W.i.c.
- Vaulted M.Bath
- TRAY CEILING
- Master Suite 16⁰ x 14⁰
- Bath
- K.S.
- Laund.
- LINEN
- BOOKSHELVES
- W.i.c.
- Bedroom 3 11⁰ x 11⁰
- Bedroom 2 11⁵ x 12⁴
- STAIRS DN.
- OPEN RAIL
- Foyer Below

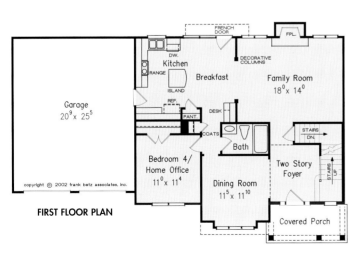

FIRST FLOOR PLAN

- Garage 20⁹ x 25⁵
- FRENCH DOOR
- Kitchen
- DW.
- RANGE
- ISLAND
- Breakfast
- DECORATIVE COLUMNS
- FPL
- Family Room 18⁰ x 14⁰
- REF.
- DESK
- PANT.
- COATS
- Bath
- STAIRS DN.
- Bedroom 4/ Home Office 11⁰ x 11⁴
- Dining Room 11⁵ x 11¹⁰
- Two Story Foyer
- STAIRS UP
- Covered Porch

copyright © 2002 frank betz associates, inc.

Rear Elevation

Plan number: FSFB02-3742

Bedrooms: 4
Baths: 3
Width: 51'-0"
Depth: 36'-4"
Main Level: 1052 sq ft
Upper Level: 1008 sq ft
Living Area: 2060 sq ft
Opt. Bonus Room 282 sq ft
PRICE CODE: **C**

© Frank Betz Associates, Inc.

SECOND FLOOR PLAN

Master Suite 16⁰ x 14¹⁰ (TRAY CEILING)
Vaulted M.Bath
SHWR.
W.i.c.
LINEN
W.i.c.
Bedroom 3 11³ x 12⁰
OPEN RAIL STAIRS DN.
LINEN
Bath
OVERLOOK
Bedroom 2 12² x 11⁹
Foyer Below
Laund.
W.i.c.
Opt. Bonus 11⁵ x 14⁹

QUAIL RIDGE

DESIGN NOTES | Quaint and timeless, the façade of the Quail Ridge is graced with dormers and a covered porch. The breakfast and family rooms are connected into one functional space, creating casual and comfortable family time. A bedroom on the main level is the perfect place for guests, and can also be used as a den. Optional bonus space upstairs opens up many possibilities for those needing a little extra space. Commuters may prefer to use this space as a home office, while the growing family may want a playroom. Every bedroom in this design is equipped with a walk-in closet, giving homeowners plenty of storage space.

Plan number: FSFB02-3682
Bedrooms: 4
Baths: 3
Width: 45'-0"
Depth: 42'-4"
Main Level: 1125 sq ft
Upper Level: 1062 sq ft
Living Area: 2187 sq ft
Opt. Bonus Room 229 sq ft
PRICE CODE: **D**

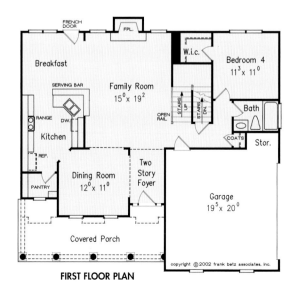

Breakfast
FRENCH DOOR
FPL
W.i.c.
Bedroom 4 11³ x 11⁰
SERVING BAR
Family Room 15⁰ x 19²
STAIRS UP STAIRS DN.
OPEN RAIL
Bath
RANGE
DW.
Kitchen
COATS
Stor.
REF.
Two Story Foyer
PANTRY
Dining Room 12⁰ x 11⁰
Garage 19⁵ x 20⁰
Covered Porch
copyright © 2002 frank betz associates, inc.

FIRST FLOOR PLAN

Rear Elevation

TO ORDER PLANS CALL TOLL FREE 888-717-3003

© Frank Betz Associates, Inc.

YARBOROUGH

DESIGN NOTES | The artistic use of stone and cedar shake accenting the façade of the Yarborough creates a warm and inviting front elevation. A two-story great room is the focal point of this design. Built-in cabinets give homeowners extra storage and fantastic decorating opportunities. The kitchen is highly functional with a prep island and built-in message center. Decorative columns divide the living and dining rooms, adding a stylish flair to this space. The main floor bedroom can easily double as a home office. Upstairs, an optional bonus area would make an ideal playroom.

SECOND FLOOR PLAN

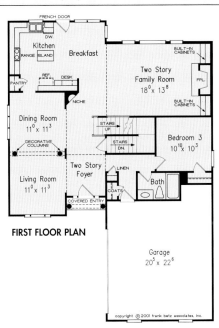

FIRST FLOOR PLAN

Rear Elevation

Plan number: FSFB02-3641	
Bedrooms:	3
Baths:	3
Width:	40'-0"
Depth:	57'-0"
Main Level:	1293 sq ft
Upper Level:	922 sq ft
Living Area:	2215 sq ft
Opt. Bonus Room	235 sq ft
PRICE CODE:	**D**

© Frank Betz Associates, Inc.

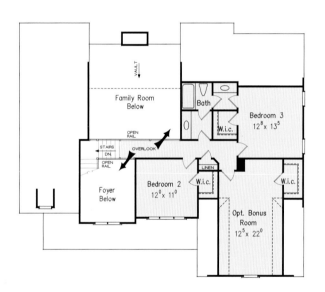

HOLLY SPRINGS

DESIGN NOTES | The Craftsman façade of the Holly Springs is eye-catching and original with its unique windows, battered columns, and varied exterior materials. A vaulted breakfast area connects to the kitchen, complete with double ovens and a serving bar. Additional niceties include an arched opening leading to the family room from the foyer and a linen closet in the master suite.

Plan number: FSFB02-3821	
Bedrooms: 4	
Baths: 3	
Width: 56'-0"	
Depth: 48'-0"	
Main Level:	1761 sq ft
Upper Level:	577 sq ft
Living Area:	2338 sq ft
Opt. Bonus Room	305 sq ft
PRICE CODE: **D**	

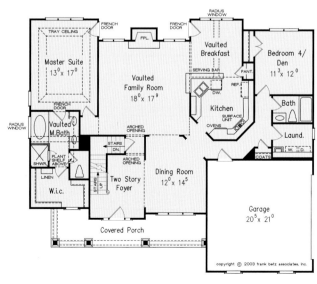

Rear Elevation

© Frank Betz Associates, Inc.

MODESTO

DESIGN NOTES | A few special added amenities give the Modesto an edge over some of its two-story rivals. The Craftsman-style columns on the front porch are a feature of today's most popular designs. Flexible spaces inside give home-owners plenty of options based on their specific needs. The main floor bedroom is also an ideal location for a study. The optional bonus area upstairs – with a sunny window seat – can be easily finished into a family recreation area, crafting room or home gym. The kitchen's island and butler's pantry make gath-erings easier, whether formal or informal.

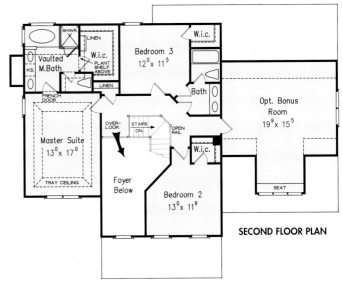

SECOND FLOOR PLAN

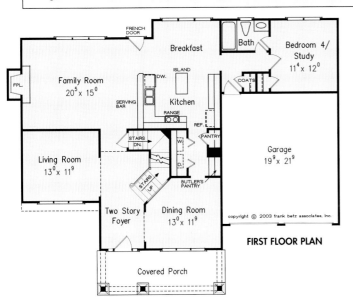

FIRST FLOOR PLAN

copyright © 2003 frank betz associates, inc.

Rear Elevation

Plan number: FSFB02-3803	
Bedrooms: 4	
Baths: 3	
Width: 56'-10"	
Depth: 45'-6"	
Main Level:	1404 sq ft
Upper Level:	959 sq ft
Living Area:	2363 sq ft
Opt. Bonus Room	374 sq ft
PRICE CODE: **D**	

© Frank Betz Associates, Inc.

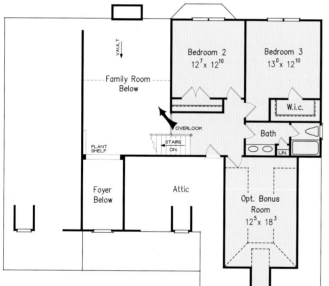

Bedroom 2
12⁷ x 12¹⁰

Bedroom 3
13⁰ x 12¹⁰

VAULT

Family Room Below

W.i.c.

OVERLOOK

Bath

PLANT SHELF

STAIRS DN.

LIN.

Foyer Below

Attic

Opt. Bonus Room
12⁵ x 18³

TULLAMORE SQUARE

DESIGN NOTES | Beautiful shingled siding and window detailing lend a New England charm to this lovely home. The great room enjoys a warm, inviting fireplace, perfect for a chilly afternoon. Entering from the back, lovely French doors open into an island kitchen and breakfast bay. Two bedrooms are upstairs, complete with a bonus room. The first floor master suite has a spacious sitting room.

SEAT

FPL

SHWR.

Vaulted M.Bath

His

Hers

LINEN

TRAY CEILING

Master Suite
13⁰ x 23⁶

Sitting Area

Vaulted Family Room
15⁰ x 19⁰

OPEN RAIL

STAIRS UP

STAIRS DN.

Two Story Foyer

FRENCH DOOR

Breakfast

SERVING BAR

DW.

Kitchen

ISLAND

RANGE

Dining Room
13⁰ x 12³

REF.

Covered Porch

Bedroom 4/ Study
12⁵ x 11⁰

PANT.

Bath

Laund.

W. D.

COATS

Garage
20⁵ x 22³

Rear Elevation

Plan number: FSFB02-3801

Bedrooms: 4

Baths: 3

Width: 55'-0"

Depth: 48'-0"

Main Level: 1805 sq ft

Upper Level: 593 sq ft

Living Area: 2398 sq ft

Opt. Bonus Room 255 sq ft

PRICE CODE: **E**

copyright © 2003 frank betz associates, inc.

TO ORDER PLANS CALL TOLL FREE 888-717-3003

© Frank Betz Associates, Inc.

FORTENBERRY

DESIGN NOTES | The needs of today's family vary from one household to the next, so the Fortenberry was created to give homeowner's choices on how they want to use their space. A main floor bedroom can be used as just that, or can be easily changed to a home office or den. Upstairs, a unique loft area with a cozy window seat makes a great place for a children's lounging area or homework station. An optional bonus room can serve a multitude of purposes, like a crafting room, exercise area or family recreation room.

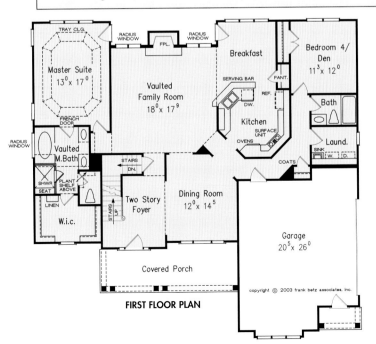

FIRST FLOOR PLAN

Master Suite 13⁰ x 17⁰
Vaulted Family Room 18⁰ x 17⁹
Breakfast
Bedroom 4/Den 11³ x 12⁰
Kitchen
Bath
Laund.
Vaulted M.Bath
W.i.c.
Two Story Foyer
Dining Room 12⁰ x 14⁵
Garage 20⁵ x 26⁰
Covered Porch

copyright © 2003 frank betz associates, inc.

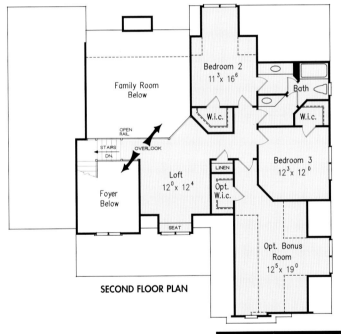

SECOND FLOOR PLAN

Family Room Below
Bedroom 2 11³ x 16⁶
Bath
W.i.c.
W.i.c.
Loft 12⁰ x 12⁴
Bedroom 3 12³ x 12⁰
Foyer Below
Opt. W.i.c.
Opt. Bonus Room 12⁵ x 19⁰
SEAT

Rear Elevation

© Frank Betz Associates, Inc.

SECOND FLOOR PLAN

Grand Room Below

PLANT SHELF

VAULT

Bedroom 3
10⁷ x 12

Sitting/ Opt. Bdrm. 5
12⁰ x 11³

TRAY CEILING

Master Suite
17⁰ x 13⁴

Bath
LINEN

OPEN RAIL

STAIRS DN.

KS.

VAULT

Bedroom 2
12⁰ x 11³

PLANT SHELF

Foyer Below

OVERLOOK

W.i.c.

Vaulted M.Bath

SHWR

LINEN

DUNHILL

DESIGN NOTES | This design has stunning curb appeal with its interesting dimension and many windows. The Dunhill is refreshingly original inside, with a vaulted grand room that is its own entity on the left side of the home. Its spread of windows and vaulted ceiling makes this area a bright and cheery room to be shared by the whole family. Telecommuters, business owners and at-home mothers will appreciate that the main floor bedroom easily converts into a home office. The master suite can be even more luxurious by opting to replace a bedroom upstairs with a private sitting area.

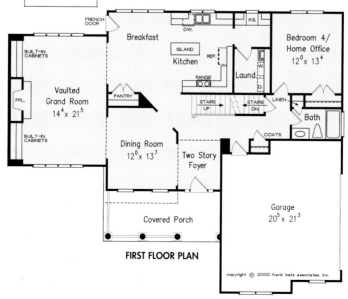

FRENCH DOOR

BUILT-IN CABINETS

Breakfast

ISLAND

Kitchen

DW.

KS.

REF.

Bedroom 4/ Home Office
12⁰ x 13⁴

W.

RANGE

Laund.

D.

LINEN

FPL

Vaulted Grand Room
14⁴ x 21⁵

PANTRY

STAIRS UP

STAIRS DN

Bath

BUILT-IN CABINETS

COATS

Dining Room
12⁰ x 13⁷

Two Story Foyer

Covered Porch

Garage
20⁵ x 21³

FIRST FLOOR PLAN

copyright © 2000 frank betz associates, inc.

Rear Elevation

Plan number: FSFB02-3560
Bedrooms: 5
Baths: 3
Width: 58'-0"
Depth: 47'-0"
Main Level: 1447 sq ft
Upper Level: 1109 sq ft
Living Area: 2556 sq ft
PRICE CODE: **D**

© Frank Betz Associates, Inc.

Southern Living
Design Collection

RANDOLPH PLACE

DESIGN NOTES | Randolph Place captures the essence of favorite country homes from the past with its columned front porch, clapboard siding and expanse of windows. Brick accents, flower boxes and shutters add the final touch for an inviting exterior. Inside, the home offers an innovative floor plan to accommodate today's family lifestyles. The grand two-story foyer opens into a formal dining room where a butler's pantry has been added for convenience. The cozy kitchen is the center of activity. A serving bar over the sink opens to the breakfast room and family room for easy family interaction. Completing the downstairs is a fourth bedroom, ideally situated as a private guest room or mother-in-law suite, with its own bath and walk-in closet. Upstairs, the master suite offers a decorative tray ceiling, separate his and her closets and a luxurious bath. Secondary bedrooms are spacious and enjoy their own vanities.

SECOND FLOOR PLAN

master bedroom 17'0"×14'1"
open to below
bedroom 12'0"×13'1"
open to below
dn.
bedroom 11'0"×11'0"

copyright ©1998 frank betz associates, inc.

breakfast 11'5"×10'0"
garage 20'9"×20'5"
kitchen 13'5"×11'11"
family room 17'9"×16'2"
bedroom 11'0"×10'9"
living 10'3"×12'0"
foyer
up
dn.
dining 13'5"×11'2"
FIRST FLOOR PLAN
covered porch

Rear Elevation

Plan number:	FSFB02-1239
Bedrooms:	4
Baths:	3
Width:	55'-4"
Depth:	55'-6"
Main Level:	1449 sq ft
Upper Level:	1154 sq ft
Living Area:	2603 sq ft
PRICE CODE:	**E**

© Frank Betz Associates, Inc.

PORT ROYAL

SECOND FLOOR PLAN

Sitting

RADIUS WINDOW

KS.

Vaulted M.Bath

TRAY CEILING

Master Suite
13⁰ x 17⁵

Family Room Below

Bedroom 2
11⁰ x 12¹⁰

SHWR

LINEN

W.i.c.

LINEN

Bath

Bedroom 4
11² x 11⁶

W.i.c.

OVERLOOK

OPEN RAIL

STAIRS DN

Bath

Bedroom 3
12⁰ x 12⁸

Foyer Below

RADIUS WINDOW

PLANT SHELF

DESIGN NOTES | A gentle mix of shingles, brick and clapboard siding lend a relaxed spirit to this spacious four-bedroom home. The wrapping front porch provides an outdoor comfort zone, yet is a mere introduction to a grand plan that offers many welcoming retreats. Built-in cabinetry frames a massive fireplace in the two-story family room—designed to take in light and views from the back property. Walls of glass allow daylight to brighten the breakfast bay, kitchen and keeping room, creating an inviting space for family members to gather. On the upper level, sleeping quarters include a luxurious master suite with a sitting bay, and three secondary bedrooms linked by a balcony bridge.

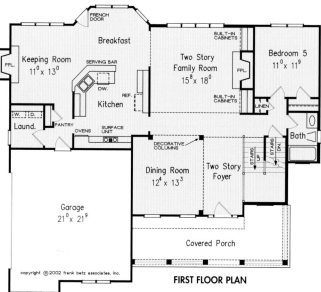

FRENCH DOOR

Breakfast

Keeping Room
11⁰ x 13⁰

FPL.

SERVING BAR

DW.

Kitchen

REF.

BUILT-IN CABINETS

Two Story Family Room
15⁸ x 18⁰

FPL.

Bedroom 5
11⁰ x 11⁹

BUILT-IN CABINETS

LINEN

W.I.D.

Laund.

PANTRY

OVENS

SURFACE UNIT

Bath

DECORATIVE COLUMNS

Dining Room
12⁴ x 13³

Two Story Foyer

STAIRS UP

STAIRS DN

Garage
21⁰ x 21⁹

Covered Porch

copyright © 2002 frank betz associates, inc.

FIRST FLOOR PLAN

Plan number: FSFB02-3724

Bedrooms: 5
Baths: 4
Width: 56'-4"
Depth: 48'-0"
Main Level: 1462 sq ft
Upper Level: 1271 sq ft
Living Area: 2733 sq ft

PRICE CODE: E

Rear Elevation

KINGSGATE

DESIGN NOTES | The Kingsgate design is carefully planned with a combination of practicality and style. Five bedrooms, four full baths and a powder room comfortably accommodate today's growing family. The main-level bedroom with a private bathroom makes a great guest suite, but also easily converts into a home office to cater to telecommuters and stay-at-home moms. The two-story great room is canopied with a coffered ceiling, adding a stylish accent to the room. The master suite's most prominent feature is its private sitting area with a vaulted ceiling and radius window.

SECOND FLOOR PLAN

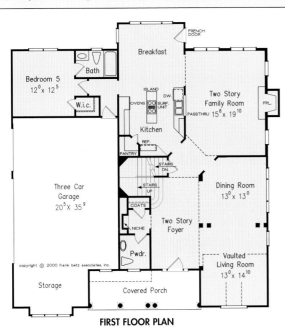

FIRST FLOOR PLAN

Rear Elevation

Plan number:	FSFB02-3580
Bedrooms:	5
Baths:	4.5
Width:	52'-4"
Depth:	55'-6"
Main Level:	1658 sq ft
Upper Level:	1600 sq ft
Living Area:	3258 sq ft
PRICE CODE:	**E**

OPTIONAL
BEDROOMS

From the sidewalk, the Guilford [page 96] design evokes the charm of a 20th-Century farmhouse. Inside, however, this ultra-flexible design takes on the excitement of a tomrrowland house, with the capacity for change and growth that our current era's lifestyles require. With formal rooms placed to the front of the plan, the Hopkins progresses to more relaxed spaces at the rear of the home, including a flexible room that easily converts from a study or den to an additional bedroom. Equipped with a full bath and an ample wardrobe, this room also accommodates a teenager or a live-in relative. More importantly, when used as guest quarters, the room grants the required privacy yet permits the visitor easy access to the casual living zone and to places where the family frequently gathers. ■

Left | Yellow polka dot walls create a whimsical retreat for a princess.

© Frank Betz Associates, Inc.

MARSHALL

Creative design and flexible space give the Marshall an edge over its one-level counterparts. A comfortable covered porch extends a warm welcome at the end of a busy day. The master suite – complete with a private sitting area – provides a peaceful place to curl up with a good book. An optional fireplace makes this space even more inviting. Separate eating areas adjoin the kitchen – a breakfast area suitable for casual meals and a dining room for more formal gatherings. Vaulted and tray ceilings in the family room and master suite give these rooms an open, spacious appeal.

Rear Elevation

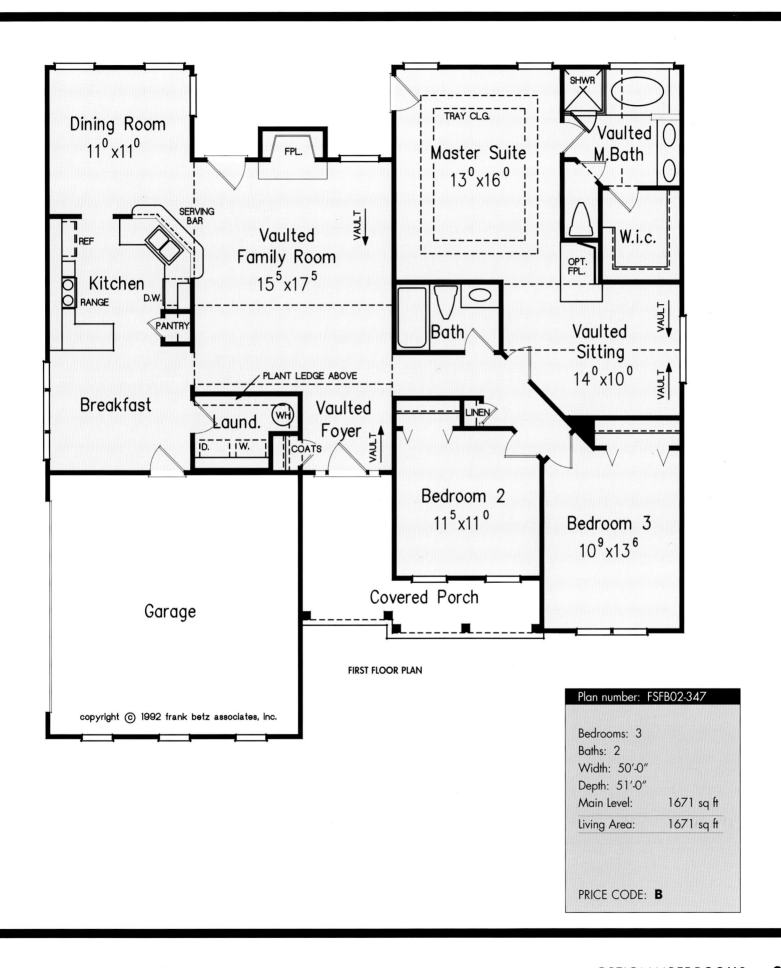

Dining Room
11⁰x11⁰

FPL.

Master Suite
13⁰x16⁰

TRAY CLG.

SHWR

Vaulted
M. Bath

SERVING BAR

REF

Kitchen

RANGE

D.W.

PANTRY

Vaulted
Family Room
15⁵x17⁵

VAULT

OPT. FPL.

W.i.c.

Bath

VAULT

Vaulted
Sitting
14⁰x10⁰

VAULT

Breakfast

PLANT LEDGE ABOVE

Laund.

WH

ID.

W.

Vaulted
Foyer

VAULT

COATS

LINEN

Bedroom 2
11⁵x11⁰

Bedroom 3
10⁹x13⁶

Garage

copyright © 1992 frank betz associates, inc.

Covered Porch

FIRST FLOOR PLAN

Plan number: FSFB02-347

Bedrooms: 3
Baths: 2
Width: 50'-0"
Depth: 51'-0"
Main Level: 1671 sq ft
Living Area: 1671 sq ft

PRICE CODE: **B**

© Frank Betz Associates, Inc.

ROSWELL

Rear Elevation

High ceilings in the foyer await your entrance into this charming floor plan. Decorative columns separate the dining and family rooms, which contribute to the openness of the home. The breakfast room is connected to the kitchen, perfect for informal dining, while the breakfast area boasts elegant windows and a French door.

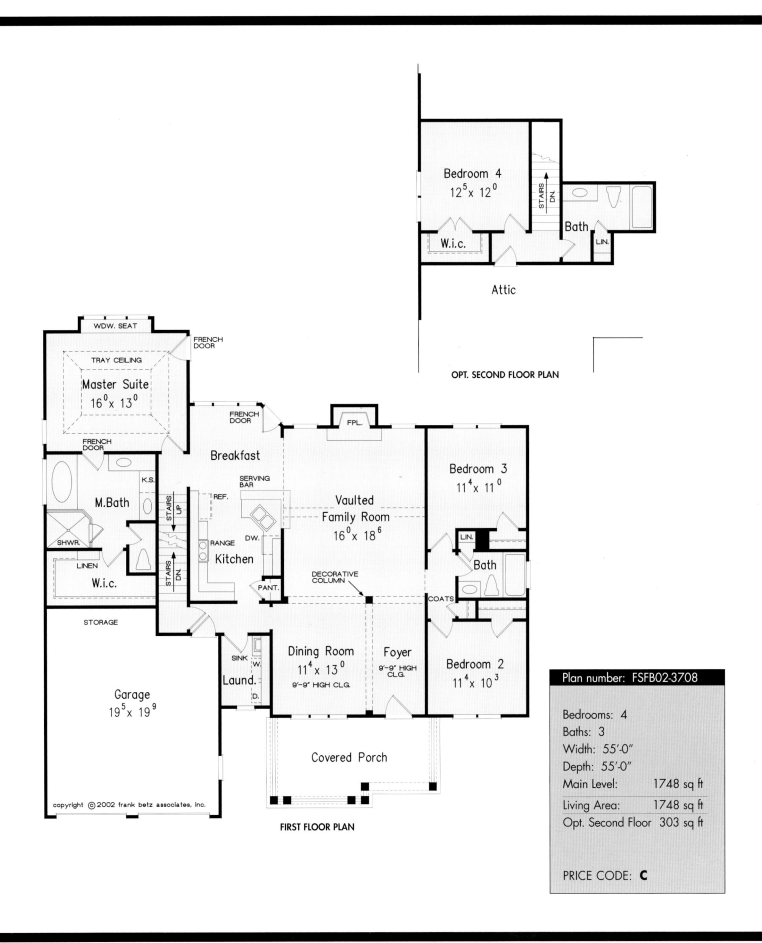

Bedroom 4
12⁵ x 12⁰

STAIRS DN.

Bath

W.i.c.

LIN.

Attic

OPT. SECOND FLOOR PLAN

WDW. SEAT

FRENCH DOOR

TRAY CEILING

Master Suite
16⁰ x 13⁰

FRENCH DOOR

FRENCH DOOR

M.Bath

K.S.

SHWR.

LINEN

W.i.c.

STORAGE

Garage
19⁵ x 19⁹

STAIRS UP

STAIRS DN.

Breakfast

SERVING BAR

REF.

RANGE

DW.

Kitchen

PANT.

FPL.

Vaulted
Family Room
16⁰ x 18⁶

DECORATIVE COLUMN

Bedroom 3
11⁴ x 11⁰

LIN.

Bath

COATS

SINK

W.

Laund.

D.

Dining Room
11⁴ x 13⁰
9'-9" HIGH CLG.

Foyer
9'-9" HIGH CLG.

Bedroom 2
11⁴ x 10³

Covered Porch

copyright © 2002 frank betz associates, inc.

FIRST FLOOR PLAN

Plan number: FSFB02-3708	
Bedrooms: 4	
Baths: 3	
Width: 55'-0"	
Depth: 55'-0"	
Main Level:	1748 sq ft
Living Area:	1748 sq ft
Opt. Second Floor	303 sq ft
PRICE CODE: **C**	

© Frank Betz Associates, Inc.

KENMORE PARK

A traditional combination of brick and siding is a backdrop for the rocking-chair front porch that adorns the front of the Kenmore Park. Oval and radius windows provide that fresh, homey appeal sought after today. Inside, a clean and simple design features three bedrooms and two baths. Optional space opens the opportunity for a fourth bedroom and third bath.

Rear Elevation

Plan number: FSFB02-3700

Bedrooms: 4
Baths: 3
Width: 62'-0"
Depth: 51'-10"
Main Level: 1769 sq ft
Living Area: 1769 sq ft
Opt. Second Floor 289 sq ft

PRICE CODE: **C**

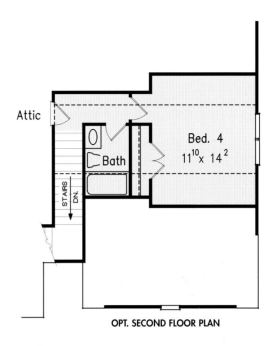

Attic

Bath

Bed. 4
11^{10} x 14^2

STAIRS DN.

OPT. SECOND FLOOR PLAN

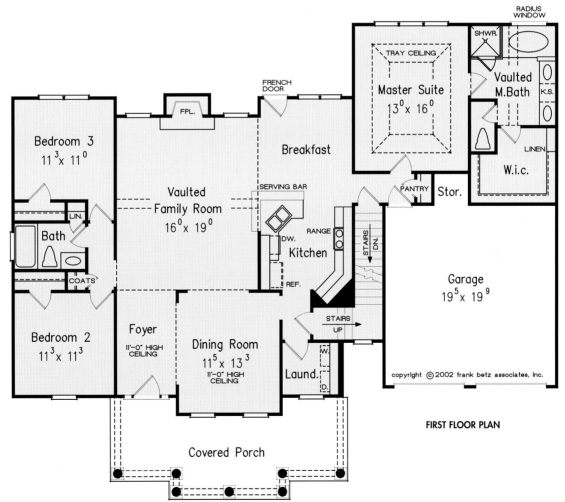

RADIUS WINDOW

SHWR.

TRAY CEILING

Master Suite
13^0 x 16^0

Vaulted M.Bath

K.S.

FRENCH DOOR

FPL.

Bedroom 3
11^3 x 11^0

Breakfast

LINEN

PANTRY   Stor.

W.i.c.

SERVING BAR

LIN.

Vaulted
Family Room
16^0 x 19^0

Bath

DW.

RANGE

Kitchen

STAIRS DN.

REF.

Garage
19^5 x 19^9

COATS

Foyer
11'-0" HIGH CEILING

Dining Room
11^5 x 13^3
11'-0" HIGH CEILING

STAIRS UP

Bedroom 2
11^3 x 11^3

W.

Laund.

D.

copyright © 2002 frank betz associates, inc.

FIRST FLOOR PLAN

Covered Porch

© Frank Betz Associates, Inc.

GUILFORD

Quaint...Timeless...Classic...all of these so accurately describe the charm that the Guilford exudes. From the cheery dormers, to the comfy front porch, to the board and batten shutters, this design steps off the streets of yesteryear. Inside, the master suite features a wall of windows with views to the rear. Two additional bedrooms share a divided bath.

Rear Elevation

TO ORDER PLANS CALL TOLL FREE 888-717-3003

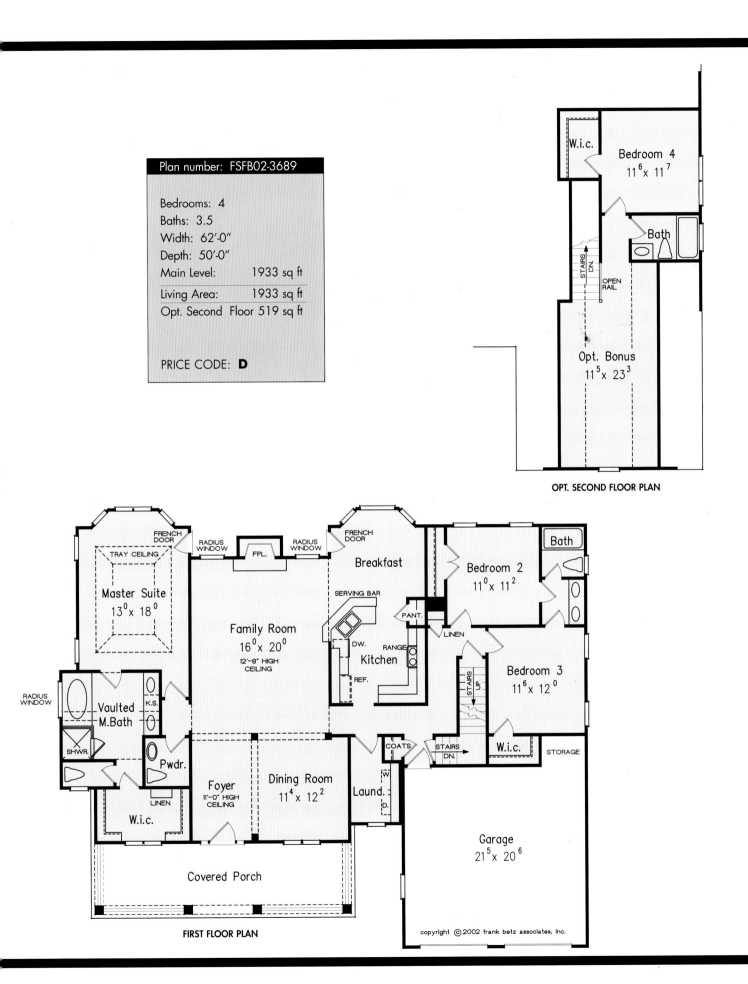

Plan number: FSFB02-3689

Bedrooms: 4
Baths: 3.5
Width: 62'-0"
Depth: 50'-0"
Main Level: 1933 sq ft
Living Area: 1933 sq ft
Opt. Second Floor 519 sq ft

PRICE CODE: **D**

W.i.c.

Bedroom 4
11⁶ x 11⁷

Bath

STAIRS DN.

OPEN RAIL

Opt. Bonus
11⁵ x 23³

OPT. SECOND FLOOR PLAN

FRENCH DOOR

RADIUS WINDOW

FPL.

RADIUS WINDOW

FRENCH DOOR

Breakfast

Bath

TRAY CEILING

Master Suite
13⁰ x 18⁰

SERVING BAR

Bedroom 2
11⁰ x 11²

PANT.

Family Room
16⁰ x 20⁰

12'-8" HIGH CEILING

DW.

RANGE

Kitchen

LINEN

RADIUS WINDOW

Vaulted
M.Bath

K.S.

REF.

Bedroom 3
11⁶ x 12⁰

STAIRS UP

SHWR.

Pwdr.

COATS

STAIRS DN.

W.i.c.

STORAGE

LINEN

W.i.c.

Foyer
11'-0" HIGH CEILING

Dining Room
11⁴ x 12²

Laund.

W. D.

Covered Porch

Garage
21⁵ x 20⁶

FIRST FLOOR PLAN

copyright © 2002 frank betz associates, inc.

PALMDALE

Special details and added extras give the Palmdale an edge over its one-level competitors. Its exterior blend of cedar shake, siding and brick come together to create a warm and welcoming façade. Step inside to find exceptional design, planning and details. A unique niche is incorporated into the foyer, providing the ideal location for that special furniture piece or artwork. Transom windows allow extra light to pour into the family room. A generously sized optional bonus area provides an additional bedroom, a home office, or exercise room.

Rear Elevation

Plan number: FSFB02-3776

Bedrooms: 4
Baths: 3.5
Width: 59'-0"
Depth: 57'-0"
Main Level: 2073 sq ft
Living Area: 2073 sq ft
Opt. Second Floor 350 sq ft

PRICE CODE: **C**

OPT. SECOND FLOOR PLAN

Bedroom 4
13^3 x 15^0

STAIRS DN.

OPEN RAIL

Bath

W.i.c.

Attic

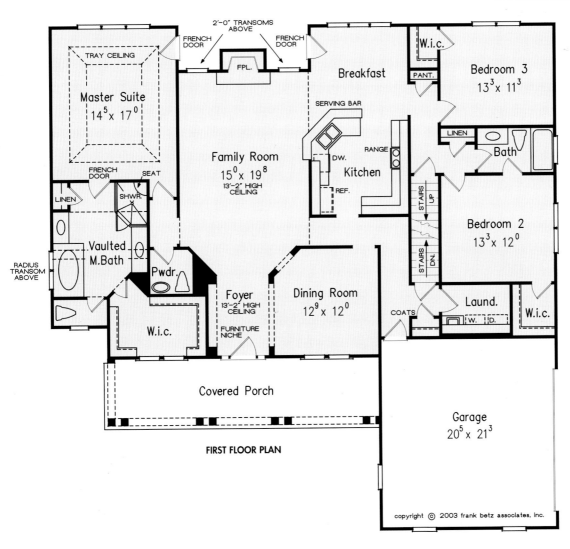

FIRST FLOOR PLAN

TRAY CEILING

Master Suite
14^5 x 17^0

FRENCH DOOR

2'-0" TRANSOMS ABOVE

FRENCH DOOR

FPL.

Breakfast

W.i.c.

PANT.

Bedroom 3
13^3 x 11^3

SERVING BAR

Family Room
15^0 x 19^8
13'-2" HIGH CEILING

DW.

Kitchen

RANGE

REF.

LINEN

Bath

FRENCH DOOR

SEAT

LINEN

SHWR.

RADIUS TRANSOM ABOVE

Vaulted M.Bath

Pwdr.

STAIRS UP

Bedroom 2
13^3 x 12^0

STAIRS DN.

W.i.c.

Foyer
13'-2" HIGH CEILING

Dining Room
12^9 x 12^0

COATS

Laund.

W. D.

W.i.c.

FURNITURE NICHE

Covered Porch

Garage
20^5 x 21^3

copyright © 2003 frank betz associates, inc.

© Frank Betz Associates, Inc.

Bedroom 4
11³ x 12⁷

W.i.c.

LIN.

STAIRS
DN.

OPEN
RAIL

Bath

Attic

OPT. SECOND FLOOR PLAN

BLOOMFIELD

DESIGN NOTES | Cedar shakes accent the façade of the Bloomfield, giving it warm and friendly curb appeal. Its split bedroom design gives privacy to the homeowner, as the master suite remains its own entity. High ceilings make the 1,769 square feet feel like more and add to the character of the home. A decorative plant shelf above the dining room provides a great decorating opportunity. This area is easily customized into a guest suite, home office, or exercise room. Extra storage space was added to the garage, keeping tools and outdoor equipment in their place.

Plan number: FSFB02-3693	
Bedrooms: 4	
Baths: 3	
Width: 61'-0"	
Depth: 47'-8"	
Main Level:	1769 sq ft
Living Area:	1769 sq ft
Opt. Second Floor	324 sq ft
PRICE CODE: **B**	

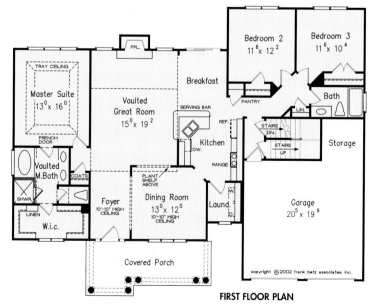

FIRST FLOOR PLAN

FPL

TRAY CEILING

Master Suite
13⁰ x 16⁰

Vaulted
Great Room
15⁰ x 19²

SERVING BAR

Breakfast

Bedroom 2
11⁶ x 12²

Bedroom 3
11⁶ x 10⁴

PANTRY

Bath

LIN.

REF.

STAIRS
DN.

STAIRS
UP

Storage

FRENCH
DOOR

Kitchen

DW.

RANGE

Vaulted
M.Bath

COATS

PLANT
SHELF
ABOVE

Foyer
10'-10" HIGH
CEILING

Dining Room
13⁰ x 12⁰
10'-10" HIGH
CEILING

Laund.

Garage
20⁵ x 19⁹

SHWR.

LINEN

W.i.c.

Covered Porch

copyright © 2002 frank betz associates, inc.

Rear Elevation

TO ORDER PLANS CALL TOLL FREE 888-717-3003

© Frank Betz Associates, Inc.

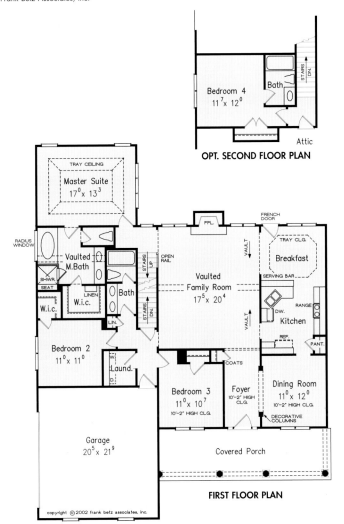

Bedroom 4
11⁷ x 12⁰

Bath

STAIRS DN

Attic

OPT. SECOND FLOOR PLAN

TRAY CEILING

Master Suite
17⁰ x 13³

RADIUS WINDOW

Vaulted M.Bath

SHWR.

SEAT

LINEN

W.i.c.

W.i.c.

Bath

LIN.

STAIRS UP

OPEN RAIL

STAIRS DN

FPL

Vaulted Family Room
17⁵ x 20⁴

VAULT

VAULT

VAULT

FRENCH DOOR

TRAY CLG.

Breakfast

SERVING BAR

Kitchen

DW.

RANGE

REF.

PANT.

Bedroom 2
11⁰ x 11⁰

W

Laund.

D

COATS

Bedroom 3
11⁰ x 10⁷

Foyer
10'-2" HIGH CLG.

10'-2" HIGH CLG.

Dining Room
11⁰ x 12⁰

DECORATIVE COLUMNS

Garage
20⁵ x 21⁹

Covered Porch

FIRST FLOOR PLAN

POWELL

DESIGN NOTES | The Powell's charming dormers and cozy front porch provide a warm welcome to its residents and visitors. A quiet master suite is tucked away on the back of the home. A vaulted ceiling in the family room adds to the spacious feel in the main living area. Thoughtful design details enhance the functionality of this home, including a handy coat closet in the foyer and the laundry room placed just off the garage. This home's character speaks through special details like a tray ceiling in the breakfast area and decorative columns in the dining room. The optional second floor makes an ideal guest suite.

Rear Elevation

Plan number:	FSFB02-3687
Bedrooms:	4
Baths:	3
Width:	50'-0"
Depth:	62'-6"
Main Level:	1792 sq ft
Living Area:	1792 sq ft
Opt. Second Floor	255 sq ft

PRICE CODE: **B**

© Frank Betz Associates, Inc.

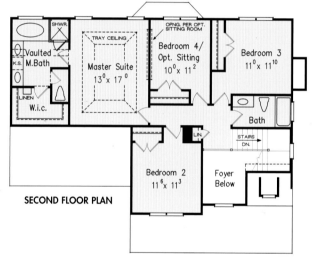

SECOND FLOOR PLAN

Vaulted M.Bath

TRAY CEILING

Master Suite 13⁰ x 17⁰

OPNG. PER OPT. SITTING ROOM

Bedroom 4/ Opt. Sitting 10⁰ x 11²

Bedroom 3 11⁰ x 11¹⁰

W.i.c.

LINEN

Bath

STAIRS DN.

Bedroom 2 11⁶ x 11³

Foyer Below

DUBOSE

DESIGN NOTES | The façade of the Dubose is relaxed and inviting with its cedar shake exterior and gabled roofline. The floor plan is well-planned and thoughtful, using every inch of its 1,918 square feet wisely. The upper floor accommodates four bedrooms, however one can be easily converted into a master suite sitting area. A laundry room and coat closet are strategically placed just off the garage, keeping shoes and coats where they belong. Additional storage space is situated in the rear of the garage, making the ideal spot for outdoor equipment.

Plan number: FSFB02-3697
Bedrooms: 4
Baths: 2.5
Width: 49'-4"
Depth: 39'-11"
Main Level: 906 sq ft
Upper Level: 1012 sq ft
Living Area: 1918 sq ft
PRICE CODE: **C**

Storage

Laund

COATS

Breakfast

FRENCH DOOR

SERVING BAR

Family Room 14⁸ x 17²

FPL.

PANT.

Garage 19⁹ x 19⁹

Kitchen

DW.

RANGE

REF.

STAIRS DN.

Dining Room 11⁶ x 11⁰

Two Story Foyer

STAIRS UP

Pwdr.

copyright © 2002 frank betz associates, inc.

FIRST FLOOR PLAN

Covered Porch

Rear Elevation

© Frank Betz Associates, Inc.

HERITAGE

DESIGN NOTES | Growing families will appreciate the many functional features that the Heritage has to offer. The main floor houses all of the common areas of the home like the kitchen, family room, breakfast area and dining room. Gentle borders create easy accessibility to and from one spot to another. All four bedrooms are on the upper level of the home. If three bedrooms are enough, one can be easily altered to become a master suite sitting area. The laundry room is located on the upper level as well, adding to the functionality of this design.

FIRST FLOOR PLAN

copyright © 2002 frank betz associates, inc.

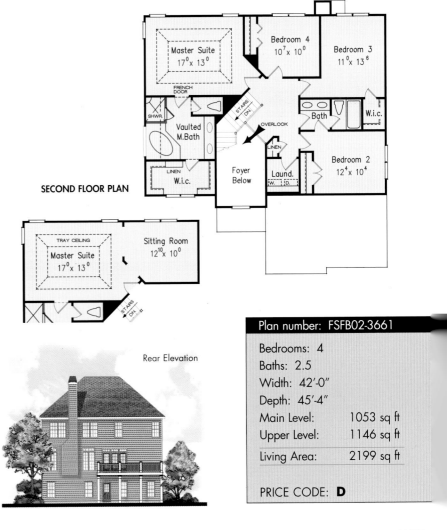

SECOND FLOOR PLAN

Rear Elevation

Plan number: FSFB02-3661
Bedrooms: 4
Baths: 2.5
Width: 42'-0"
Depth: 45'-4"
Main Level: 1053 sq ft
Upper Level: 1146 sq ft
Living Area: 2199 sq ft

PRICE CODE: **D**

© Frank Betz Associates, Inc.

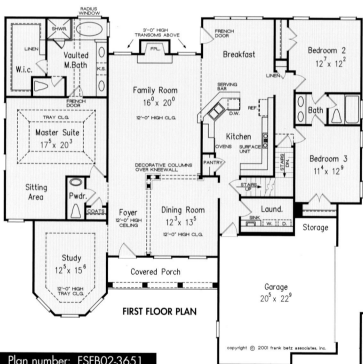

FIRST FLOOR PLAN

Family Room
16⁰ x 20⁰
12'-0" HIGH CLG.

Breakfast

Bedroom 2
12⁷ x 12²

Bath

Bedroom 3
11⁴ x 12⁹

Kitchen

Master Suite
17⁵ x 20³

Sitting Area

Vaulted M.Bath

W.i.c.

Pwdr.

Study
12⁵ x 15⁶
12'-0" HIGH TRAY CLG.

Foyer
12'-0" HIGH CEILING

Dining Room
12³ x 13⁵
12'-0" HIGH CLG.

Laund.

Storage

Covered Porch

Garage
20⁵ x 22⁹

copyright © 2001 frank betz associates, inc.

NATHANIEL

DESIGN NOTES | Beauty is in the details! The Nathaniel has many of the added extras that make a house a home. A secluded sitting area is designed into the master suite giving the homeowner a quiet spot to unwind. Decorative columns and a knee wall gently define the dining room. Transom windows allow natural light to beam into the family room. Double ovens in the kitchen add ease to entertaining and meal preparation. A handy sink is incorporated into the laundry room. Finishing the optional second floor adds a fourth bedroom and third full bath to the home.

Bedroom 4
12⁴ x 14⁶

Attic

Bath

W.i.c.

OPT. SECOND FLOOR PLAN

Rear Elevation

Plan number: FSFB02-3651

Bedrooms: 4

Baths: 3.5

Width: 62'-0"

Depth: 58'-0"

Main Level: 2331 sq ft

Living Area: 2331 sq ft

Opt. Second Floor 360 sq ft

PRICE CODE: **D**

© Frank Betz Associates, Inc.

GREENVILLE

DESIGN NOTES | Shuttered windows, siding and a lovely covered wraparound front porch add a quaint Southern charm to this traditional home. The kitchen features a serving island which opens into a breakfast bay featuring a French door that exits into the back yard. A spacious family room with see-through fireplace completes the main floor. Upstairs, four bedrooms provide ample living space.

SECOND FLOOR PLAN

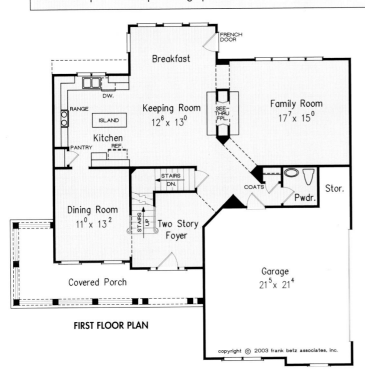

FIRST FLOOR PLAN

Rear Elevation

Plan number: FSFB02-3779	
Bedrooms:	4
Baths:	2.5
Width:	50'-0"
Depth:	49'-0"
Main Level:	1141 sq ft
Upper Level:	1202 sq ft
Living Area:	2343 sq ft
PRICE CODE:	**D**

GLENBROOKE

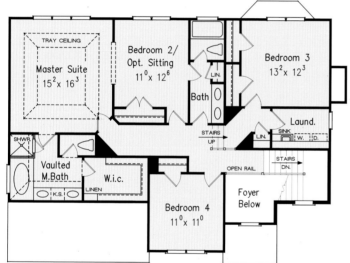

SECOND FLOOR PLAN

Master Suite 15² x 16³ · TRAY CEILING

Bedroom 2/ Opt. Sitting 11⁰ x 12⁶

Bedroom 3 13² x 12³

Bath · LIN.

Laund.

Vaulted M.Bath · SHWR. · K.S. · LINEN · W.i.c.

STAIRS UP · LIN. · SINK W. D.

OPEN RAIL · STAIRS DN.

Bedroom 4 11⁰ x 11⁰

Foyer Below

DESIGN NOTES | The Glenbrooke is a very smart design, giving the homeowner options on how they want to use their space. The bedroom on the main level of the home can remain as such, but can also make an ideal guest room or be easily converted into a home office. Another bedroom on the upper level can also be a generous sitting area adjoining the master suite. A laundry room – complete with a handy sink – is designed into the upper floor, accessible to all of the main bedrooms. The family room is accentuated with a stunning coffered ceiling, adding an interesting element to the room.

Plan number: **FSFB02-3788**

Bedrooms: 5
Baths: 3
Width: 50'-4"
Depth: 37'-9"
Main Level: 1108 sq ft
Upper Level: 1253 sq ft
Living Area: 2361 sq ft

PRICE CODE: **D**

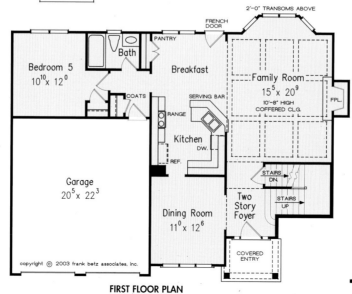

FIRST FLOOR PLAN

2'-0" TRANSOMS ABOVE

FRENCH DOOR · PANTRY

Bedroom 5 10¹⁰ x 12⁰

Bath

Breakfast

Family Room 15⁵ x 20⁹ · 10'-8" HIGH COFFERED CLG. · FPL.

COATS · SERVING BAR

RANGE

Kitchen · DW. · REF.

Garage 20⁵ x 22³

Dining Room 11⁰ x 12⁶

STAIRS DN. · STAIRS UP

Two Story Foyer

COVERED ENTRY

copyright © 2003 frank betz associates, inc.

Rear Elevation

TO ORDER PLANS CALL TOLL FREE 888-717-3003

© Frank Betz Associates, Inc.

HICKORY GROVE

DESIGN NOTES | The cottage-like appeal of the Hickory Grove is achieved by combining stone and cedar shake, accenting them with board-and-batten siding. The design inside is equally unique. The master suite enjoys the privacy of the entire main floor, and features a cozy window seat accented by decorative columns. Additional bedrooms are located in the lower level of the home. A keeping room is situated next to the kitchen, making the ideal location for casual family time, as well as entertaining. A fourth bedroom or home office can be easily incorporated by finishing the available second floor.

LOWER LEVEL PLAN

MAIN LEVEL PLAN

copyright © 2003 frank betz associates, inc.

OPT. SECOND FLOOR PLAN

Rear Elevation

Plan number: FSFB02-3800

Bedrooms: 4

Baths: 3.5

Width: 54'-0"

Depth: 63'-6"

Main Level: 1977 sq ft

Lower Level: 940 sq ft

Living Area: 2917 sq ft

Opt. Second Floor 260 sq ft

PRICE CODE: **E**

BONUS
ROOMS

Perhaps the most popular flex space in today's home is the bonus room because of its versatility. In larger homes, the bonus space can offer enough square footage for a home theater or media center. Or the space can flex to a recreation area, a reading room or a place for computers. Kids can go there to let off steam or study for the next exam. A great bonus room offers both privacy and space for whatever task is at hand, so the mood of the room can change in addition to its architecture and style. The Brookhaven [Left] features a sizeable bonus area above the garage. Linked to two secondary bedrooms and a compartmented bath, the bonus room enhances the livability of the upper level, and creates a vivid opportunity for a game room or, with an ample built-in wardrobe, a teenager's room. ■

Left | This bonus room becomes the perfect recreation space for billiard tournaments and board games.

© Frank Betz Associates, Inc.

SUMMERBROOKE

First-time homeowners and retirees love the easy, one-level living provided by the Summerbrooke. The master suite is privately situated on the right side of the home. The dining room is defined by a decorative column, maintaining an open and spacious living area. No need to move when extra space is needed – an optional bedroom, bath and bonus room are ready to finish whenever you are.

Rear Elevation

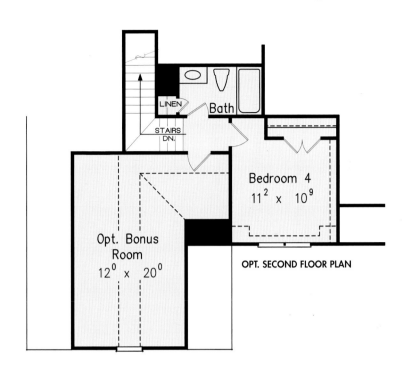

Opt. Bonus
Room
12⁰ x 20⁰

LINEN

Bath

STAIRS
DN.

Bedroom 4
11² x 10⁹

OPT. SECOND FLOOR PLAN

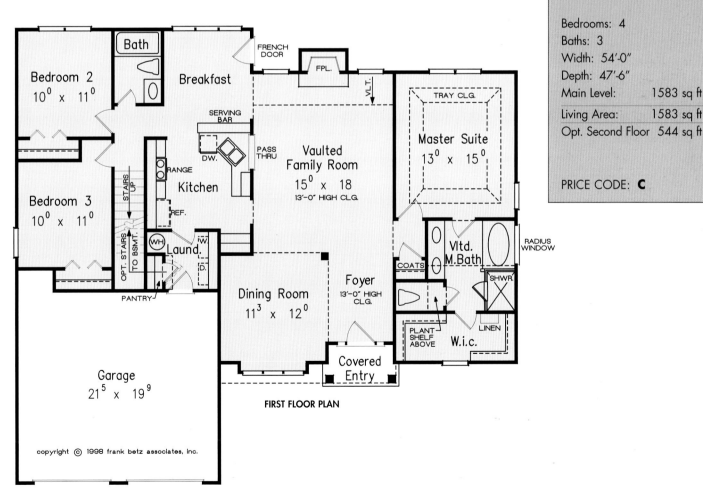

Bath

Bedroom 2
10⁰ x 11⁰

Breakfast

FRENCH
DOOR

FPL.

VLT.

TRAY CLG.

Master Suite
13⁰ x 15⁰

SERVING
BAR

DW.

PASS
THRU

RANGE

Kitchen

REF.

STAIRS UP

OPT. STAIRS
TO BSMT.

Bedroom 3
10⁰ x 11⁰

Vaulted
Family Room
15⁰ x 18
13'-0" HIGH CLG.

RADIUS
WINDOW

WH

W

Laund.

D

PANTRY

Dining Room
11³ x 12⁰

Foyer
13'-0" HIGH
CLG.

COATS

Vltd.
M.Bath

SHWR.

LINEN

PLANT
SHELF
ABOVE

W.i.c.

Garage
21⁵ x 19⁹

Covered
Entry

FIRST FLOOR PLAN

Plan number: FSFB02-1217

Bedrooms: 4
Baths: 3
Width: 54'-0"
Depth: 47'-6"
Main Level: 1583 sq ft
Living Area: 1583 sq ft
Opt. Second Floor 544 sq ft

PRICE CODE: **C**

© Frank Betz Associates, Inc.

BRENTWOOD

Brick and stone set off by multi-pane windows highlight the street presence of this classic home. A sheltered entry leads to a two-story foyer and wide interior vistas that extend to the back property. Rooms in the public zone are open, allowing the spaces to flex for planned events as well as family gatherings. At the heart of the home, the vaulted family room frames a fireplace with tall windows that bring in natural light. The main-level master suite boasts a tray ceiling, while two upper-level bedrooms are connected by a balcony bridge that overlooks the foyer and family room.

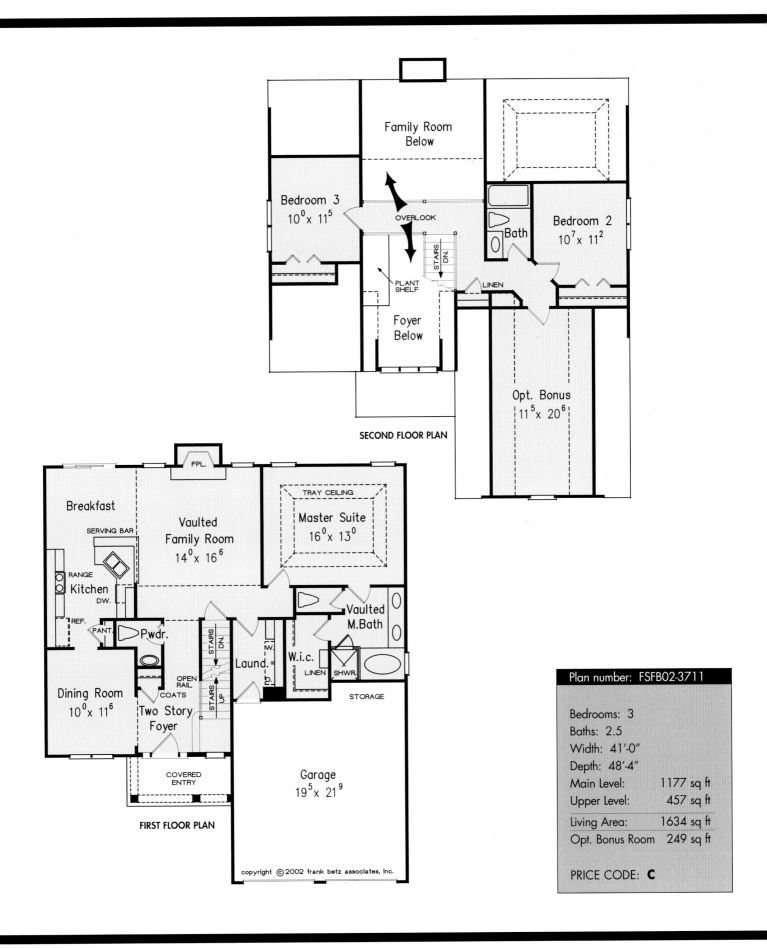

Family Room
Below

Bedroom 3
10⁰ x 11⁵

OVERLOOK

STAIRS DN.

Bath

Bedroom 2
10⁷ x 11²

PLANT SHELF

LINEN

Foyer
Below

Opt. Bonus
11⁵ x 20⁶

SECOND FLOOR PLAN

FPL.

Breakfast

TRAY CEILING

Vaulted
Family Room
14⁰ x 16⁶

Master Suite
16⁰ x 13⁰

SERVING BAR

RANGE

Kitchen

DW.

REF.

PANT.

Pwdr.

STAIRS DN.

Laund.

Vaulted
M.Bath

W.i.c.

LINEN

SHWR.

STORAGE

OPEN RAIL

COATS

Dining Room
10⁰ x 11⁶

STAIRS UP

Two Story
Foyer

Garage
19⁵ x 21⁹

COVERED
ENTRY

FIRST FLOOR PLAN

copyright © 2002 frank betz associates, inc.

Plan number: FSFB02-3711	
Bedrooms:	3
Baths:	2.5
Width:	41'-0"
Depth:	48'-4"
Main Level:	1177 sq ft
Upper Level:	457 sq ft
Living Area:	1634 sq ft
Opt. Bonus Room	249 sq ft
PRICE CODE:	**C**

SOUTHLAND HILLS

Everyone will appreciate the attentive design of the Southland Hills. Cheery dormers grace the exterior of the home and invite you in to see more. Each bedroom is buffered from the others, providing personal space for each resident. The master suite is designed as its own entity, tucked away off the breakfast area, creating a private haven for the homeowner. Additional bedrooms are separated by a bath and a laundry room. A handy coat closet is tucked away in the foyer. A fourth bedroom or home office is readily available by opting to finish the optional bonus area.

Rear Elevation

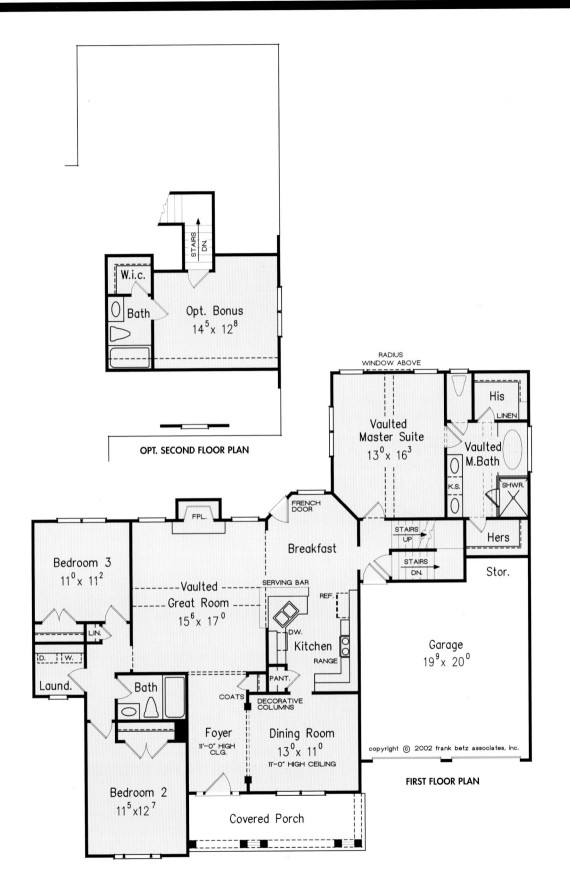

OPT. SECOND FLOOR PLAN

W.i.c.

Bath

Opt. Bonus
14⁵ x 12⁸

STAIRS DN.

RADIUS WINDOW ABOVE

Vaulted
Master Suite
13⁰ x 16³

His

LINEN

Vaulted
M.Bath

K.S.

SHWR.

FRENCH DOOR

FPL.

Breakfast

Bedroom 3
11⁰ x 11²

STAIRS UP

STAIRS DN.

Hers

Stor.

LIN.

Vaulted
Great Room
15⁶ x 17⁰

SERVING BAR

REF.

D. W.

DW.

Laund.

Kitchen

RANGE

Garage
19⁹ x 20⁰

Bath

PANT.

COATS

DECORATIVE COLUMNS

Foyer
11'-0" HIGH CLG.

Dining Room
13⁰ x 11⁰
11'-0" HIGH CEILING

Bedroom 2
11⁵ x 12⁷

Covered Porch

copyright © 2002 frank betz associates, inc.

FIRST FLOOR PLAN

Plan number: FSFB02-3747

Bedrooms: 3
Baths: 3
Width: 58'-0"
Depth: 54'-6"

Main Level:	1725 sq ft
Living Area:	1725 sq ft
Opt. Second Floor	256 sq ft

PRICE CODE: **C**

LINCOLN PARK

Shutters, shingles and siding wrap the familiar colonial lines of this country cottage with a sweet disposition. Grand arches and columns frame the foyer and gallery, flanked by well-defined formal rooms. At the heart of the home, a spacious vaulted family room yields generous views of the backyard. Built-in cabinetry and a hearth create an ambience that is right at home with the scenery. A serving bar unites the living space with the kitchen and breakfast area, which leads outdoors. The central gallery hall leads to an office suite with wardrobe space—an ideal arrangement for a guest room.

Rear Elevation

TO ORDER PLANS CALL TOLL FREE 888-717-3003

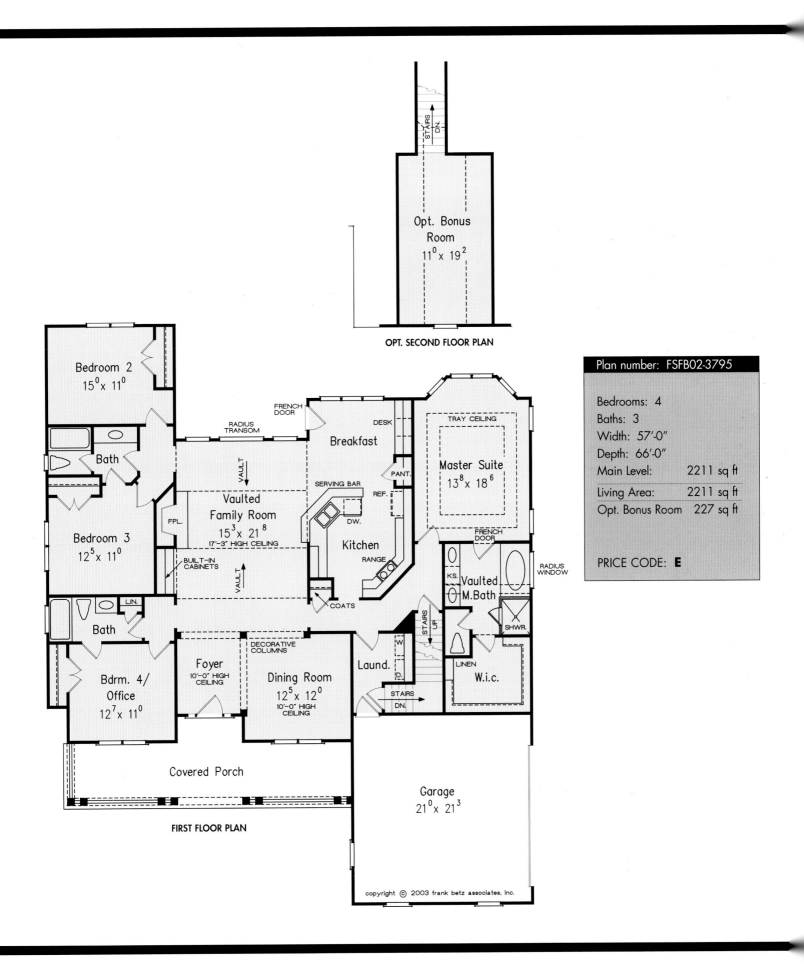

Opt. Bonus
Room
11⁰ x 19²

OPT. SECOND FLOOR PLAN

Bedroom 2
15⁰ x 11⁰

FRENCH DOOR

RADIUS TRANSOM

DESK

Breakfast

TRAY CEILING

Master Suite
13⁸ x 18⁶

Bath

VAULT

PANT.

SERVING BAR

Vaulted
Family Room
15³ x 21⁸
17'-3" HIGH CEILING

REF.

FPL.

Kitchen

DW.

FRENCH DOOR

RADIUS WINDOW

Bedroom 3
12⁵ x 11⁰

BUILT-IN CABINETS

VAULT

RANGE

Vaulted
M.Bath

KS.

LIN.

COATS

Bath

SHWR.

STAIRS UP

W.

LINEN

Bdrm. 4/
Office
12⁷ x 11⁰

Foyer
10'-0" HIGH CEILING

DECORATIVE COLUMNS

Dining Room
12⁵ x 12⁰
10'-0" HIGH CEILING

Laund.

D.

STAIRS DN.

W.i.c.

Covered Porch

Garage
21⁰ x 21³

FIRST FLOOR PLAN

copyright © 2003 frank betz associates, inc.

Plan number: FSFB02-3795

Bedrooms: 4
Baths: 3
Width: 57'-0"
Depth: 66'-0"
Main Level: 2211 sq ft
Living Area: 2211 sq ft
Opt. Bonus Room 227 sq ft

PRICE CODE: **E**

KINGSPORT

Board-and-batten siding and carriage garage doors create that cottage appeal that so many of today's homeowners are in search of. The Kingsport is as warm and welcoming inside as it is outside. The kitchen area is bright and cheery with a bay window in the breakfast area. This space caters to casual family time with a cozy keeping room connected to it. Transom windows in the breakfast and keeping rooms allow the extra light to pour in. An optional second floor provides the opportunity for a fourth bedroom, as well as additional space ideal for a customized playroom, craft room or exercise area.

Rear Elevation

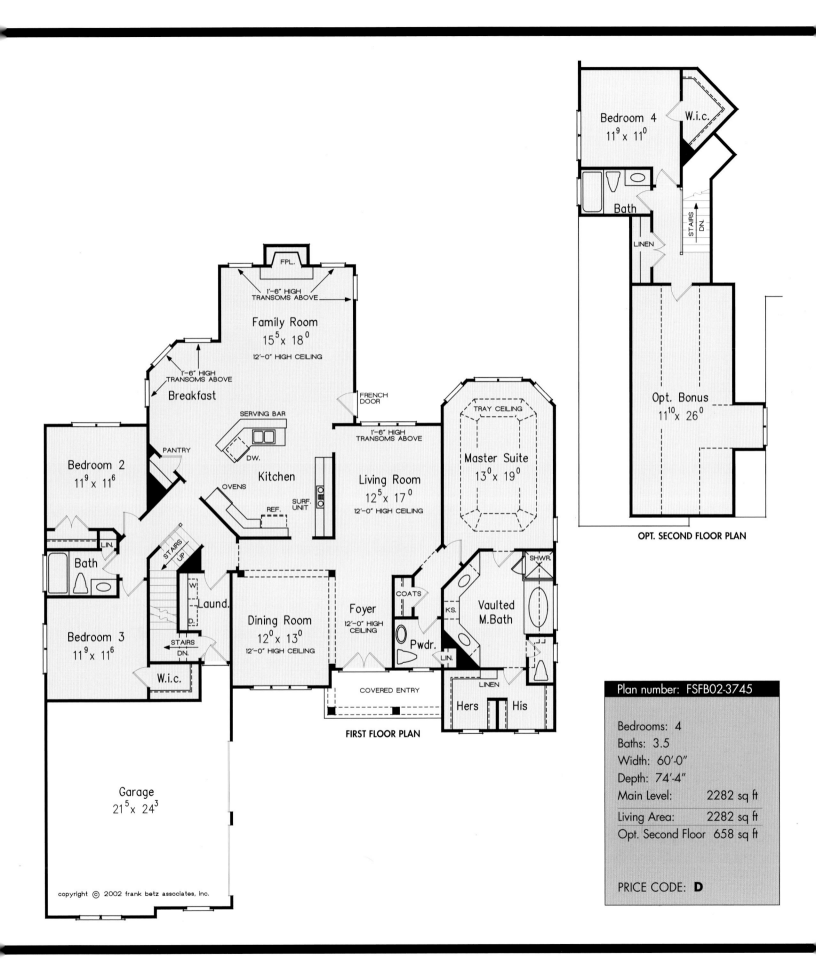

Family Room
15⁵ x 18⁰
12'-0" HIGH CEILING

1'-6" HIGH TRANSOMS ABOVE

1'-6" HIGH TRANSOMS ABOVE

Breakfast

FPL.

FRENCH DOOR

SERVING BAR

DW.

Bedroom 2
11⁹ x 11⁶

PANTRY

Kitchen

OVENS

REF.

SURF. UNIT

Living Room
12⁵ x 17⁰
12'-0" HIGH CEILING

1'-6" HIGH TRANSOMS ABOVE

TRAY CEILING

Master Suite
13⁰ x 19⁰

LIN.

Bath

STAIRS UP

W   D

Laund.

STAIRS DN.

Bedroom 3
11⁹ x 11⁶

W.i.c.

Dining Room
12⁰ x 13⁰
12'-0" HIGH CEILING

Foyer
12'-0" HIGH CEILING

COATS

Pwdr.

K.S.

SHWR.

Vaulted M.Bath

LIN.

LINEN

COVERED ENTRY

Hers   His

FIRST FLOOR PLAN

Garage
21⁵ x 24³

Bedroom 4
11⁹ x 11⁰

W.i.c.

Bath

STAIRS DN.

LINEN

Opt. Bonus
11¹⁰ x 26⁰

OPT. SECOND FLOOR PLAN

Plan number: FSFB02-3745

Bedrooms: 4
Baths: 3.5
Width: 60'-0"
Depth: 74'-4"

Main Level:	2282 sq ft
Living Area:	2282 sq ft
Opt. Second Floor	658 sq ft

PRICE CODE: **D**

FINLEY

Our Finley design offers some special amenities seldom found in ranch designs. The kitchen features a large island with a surface unit and serving bar. It leads to a private covered porch on the back of the home. We gave the master suite its own large sitting area with a fireplace. One secondary bedroom enjoys a vaulted ceiling for a spacious feel. We created an optional fourth bedroom over the kitchen, perfect for an in-law or teen suite.

Rear Elevation

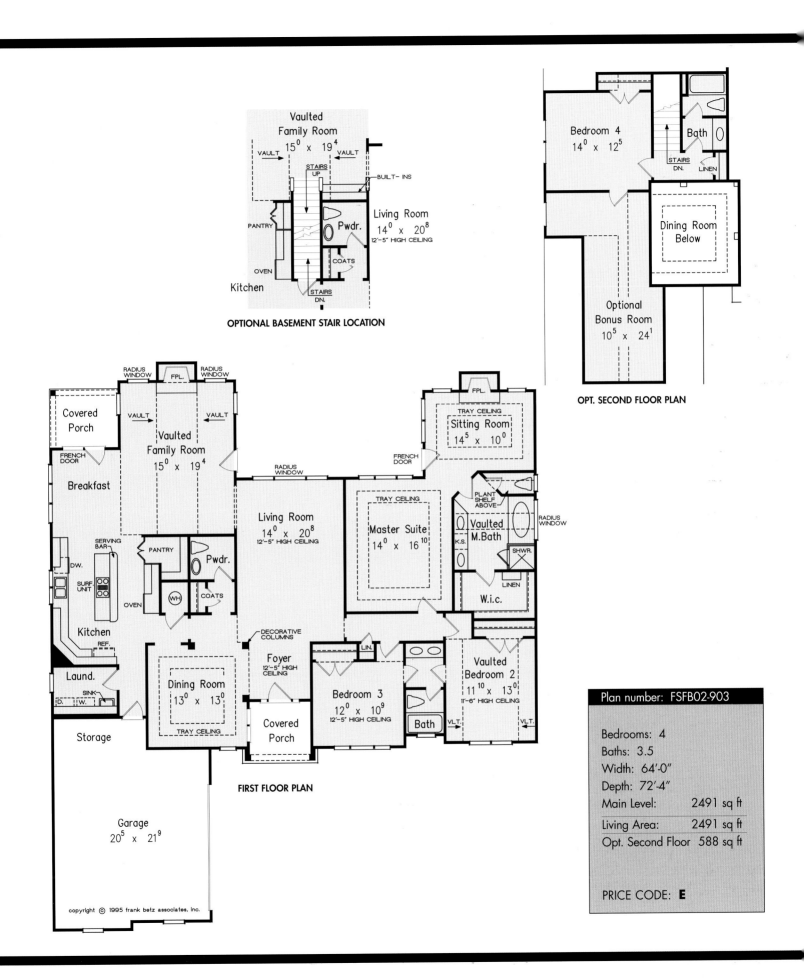

Vaulted
Family Room
15^0 x 19^4

VAULT   VAULT

STAIRS
UP

BUILT- INS

PANTRY

Living Room
14^0 x 20^8
12'-5" HIGH CEILING

Pwdr.

COATS

OVEN

Kitchen

STAIRS
DN.

OPTIONAL BASEMENT STAIR LOCATION

Bedroom 4
14^0 x 12^5

Bath

STAIRS
DN.

LINEN

Dining Room
Below

Optional
Bonus Room
10^5 x 24^1

OPT. SECOND FLOOR PLAN

RADIUS
WINDOW   FPL.   RADIUS
WINDOW

Covered
Porch

VAULT   VAULT

FPL.

TRAY CEILING

FRENCH
DOOR

Sitting Room
14^5 x 10^0

Vaulted
Family Room
15^0 x 19^4

RADIUS
WINDOW

FRENCH
DOOR

Breakfast

PLANT
SHELF
ABOVE

RADIUS
WINDOW

SERVING
BAR

Living Room
14^0 x 20^8
12'-5" HIGH CEILING

TRAY CEILING

Vaulted
M.Bath

DW.

PANTRY

Pwdr.

Master Suite
14^0 x 16^{10}

K.S.

SHWR.

SURF.
UNIT

OVEN

WH

COATS

LINEN

Kitchen

W.i.c.

REF.

Laund.

DECORATIVE
COLUMNS

Foyer
12'-5" HIGH
CEILING

LIN.

SINK

D.   W.

Dining Room
13^0 x 13^0

Bedroom 3
12^0 x 10^9
12'-5" HIGH CEILING

Vaulted
Bedroom 2
11^{10} x 13^0
11'-6" HIGH CEILING

Storage

TRAY CEILING

Covered
Porch

Bath

VLT.

VLT.

FIRST FLOOR PLAN

Garage
20^5 x 21^9

copyright © 1995 frank betz associates, inc.

Plan number: FSFB02-903
Bedrooms: 4
Baths: 3.5
Width: 64'-0"
Depth: 72'-4"
Main Level: 2491 sq ft
Living Area: 2491 sq ft
Opt. Second Floor 588 sq ft
PRICE CODE: **E**

© Frank Betz Associates, Inc.

BROADMOOR

DESIGN NOTES | Quaint and charming – outside and in – the Broadmoor combines function with beauty to make a wonderful home. The courtyard entry leads to a stunning two-story foyer. A vaulted dining room demands attention with its unique ceiling angles. The great room, breakfast area and kitchen are all connected making conversation and traffic flow effortless. The laundry room and a coat closet are thoughtfully placed just off the garage, keeping coats and shoes in their place. An optional bonus area upstairs has endless possibilities. This could be the ideal playroom, fitness area or home office.

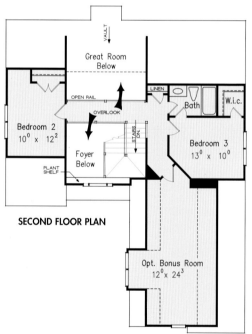

SECOND FLOOR PLAN

Plan number: FSFB02-1088	
Bedrooms:	3
Baths:	2.5
Width:	41'-6"
Depth:	54'-4"
Main Level:	1179 sq ft
Upper Level:	479 sq ft
Living Area:	1658 sq ft
Opt. Bonus Room	338 sq ft
PRICE CODE:	**B**

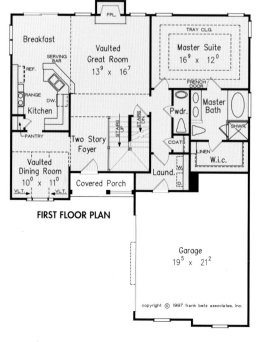

FIRST FLOOR PLAN

copyright © 1997 frank betz associates, inc.

Rear Elevation

TO ORDER PLANS CALL TOLL FREE 888-717-3003

© Frank Betz Associates, Inc.

LAKE FOREST

DESIGN NOTES | Enter the Lake Forest and you'll be greeted with a bright, welcoming atmosphere. High ceilings and radius windows generate an open and roomy feeling in the main living area. Backyard views can be enjoyed from every room on the back of this home. The split bedroom design is carefully planned, giving homeowners privacy in their master suite. Special details like decorative columns, plant shelves and tray ceilings give this home personality. The possibilities are endless with an optional bonus area over the garage, making the perfect home office, crafting area or playroom.

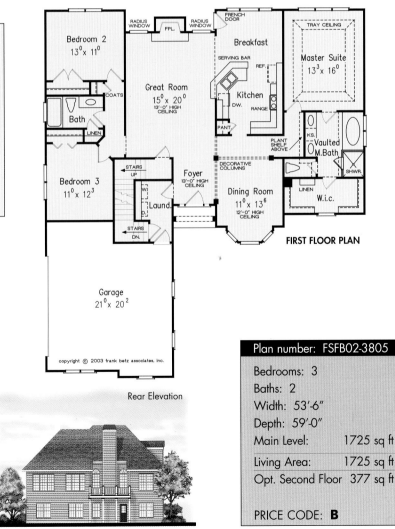

FIRST FLOOR PLAN

copyright © 2003 frank betz associates, inc.

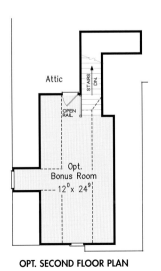

OPT. SECOND FLOOR PLAN

Rear Elevation

Plan number: **FSFB02-3805**

Bedrooms: 3
Baths: 2
Width: 53'-6"
Depth: 59'-0"
Main Level: 1725 sq ft
Living Area: 1725 sq ft
Opt. Second Floor 377 sq ft

PRICE CODE: **B**

STONEHEATH

DESIGN NOTES | The Stoneheath's clever combination of stone with board-and-batten siding creates that friendly curb appeal that many of today's homeowners are in search of. Guests will appreciate the covered entry on rainy days. Ideal for entertaining, the breakfast, living and dining rooms inconspicuously connect to create easy traffic flow from one room to the next. Just off the garage, a handy sink is designed into the laundry room, making the perfect stopping point to clean up before proceeding inside. An optional bonus room is available that easily finishes into a fourth bedroom or children's recreation room.

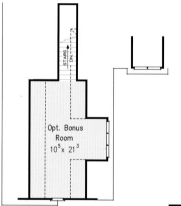

OPT. SECOND FLOOR PLAN

Opt. Bonus Room 10⁵ x 21³

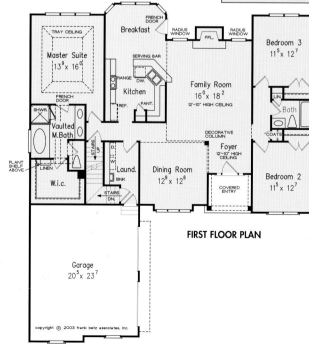

FIRST FLOOR PLAN

Breakfast · Master Suite 13⁹ x 16⁰ · Kitchen · Family Room 16⁰ x 18² · Bedroom 3 11⁵ x 12⁷ · Vaulted M.Bath · Bath · Foyer · Dining Room 12⁹ x 12⁶ · Bedroom 2 11⁵ x 12⁷ · Laund. · W.i.c. · Covered Entry · Garage 20⁵ x 23⁷

copyright © 2003 frank betz associates, inc.

Plan number:	FSFB02-3814
Bedrooms:	3
Baths:	2
Width:	54'-0"
Depth:	61'-6"
Main Level:	1750 sq ft
Living Area:	1750 sq ft
Opt. Second Floor	324 sq ft
PRICE CODE:	**B**

Rear Elevation

TO ORDER PLANS CALL TOLL FREE 888-717-3003

© Frank Betz Associates, Inc.

LYTHAM

DESIGN NOTES | Board-and-batten shutters and fieldstone accents give the Lytham the cottage-like appeal that is so sought after by today's homeowner. Just inside the covered entry, decorative columns enhance the formal dining room. Vaulted ceilings in the family room maintain an open and spacious feel throughout the main floor. Residents of the master suite will enjoy the generously sized walk-in closet. Two bedrooms share a bath on the second floor of the home. Finishing the available bonus space adds nearly 300 square feet to this design, leaving homeowners with endless possibilities on how to use this space.

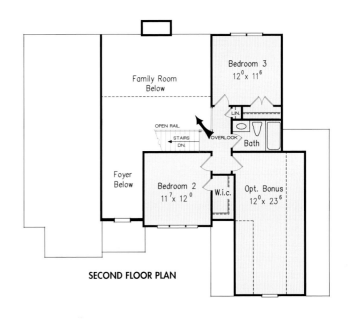

SECOND FLOOR PLAN

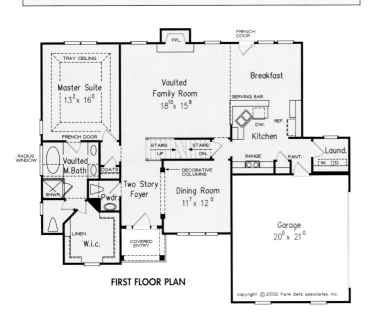

FIRST FLOOR PLAN

copyright © 2002 frank betz associates, Inc.

Rear Elevation

Plan number: **FSFB02-3703**

Bedrooms: 3
Baths: 2.5
Width: 53'-0"
Depth: 45'-10"
Main Level: 1415 sq ft
Upper Level: 448 sq ft
Living Area: 1863 sq ft
Opt. Bonus Room 297 sq ft
PRICE CODE: **C**

Southern Living
Design Collection

LANGSTON

© Frank Betz Associates, Inc.

DESIGN NOTES | Inside, high ceilings and an open floor plan make this home large and roomy. The family room is graced by a wall of windows, inviting fireplace and vaulted ceiling. The master bedroom features a tray ceiling and expansive bath with a separate tub and shower and a large walk-in closet. The Langston also offers a roomy optional bonus room with its own bath and a walk-in closet – the perfect get-away for an at-home office, game room or fourth bedroom.

opt. bonus room
11'0"x19'0"

dn.

OPT. SECOND FLOOR PLAN

breakfast
9'8"x9'

master bedroom
13'10"x16'10"

kitchen
11'8"x11'4"

living room
15'6"x20'

bedroom
11'x11'

bedroom
11'2"x11'6"

up

dining
11'3"x12'

foyer

dn.

garage
22'11"x19'4"

FIRST FLOOR PLAN

copyright © 1999 frank betz associates, inc.

Plan number: **FSFB02-1235**

Bedrooms: 3

Baths: 2.5

Width: 56'-0"

Depth: 60'-0"

Main Level: 1910 sq ft

Living Area: 1910 sq ft

Opt. Second Floor 354 sq ft

PRICE CODE: **D**

Rear Elevation

TO ORDER PLANS CALL TOLL FREE 888-717-3003

© Frank Betz Associates, Inc.

FAIRGREEN

DESIGN NOTES | A grouping of cedar shake, brick and copper accents culminate to create a warm and welcoming façade on the Fairgreen. Inconspicuous room borders make this a dream design for the entertainer. Many of the main common areas of this home are defined only by decorative columns, making traffic flow effortless from one room to the other. An optional bonus area upstairs gives the homeowner many choices on how to use the extra space, a fourth bedroom, playroom or exercise area are all possibilities.

SECOND FLOOR PLAN

W.i.c.
Bedroom 3
11⁰ x 11⁰
Bath
TRAY CEILING
Master Suite
17⁰ x 13⁰
W.i.c.
FRENCH DOOR
LIN.
Bedroom 2
10² x 11²
Laund.
W. D.
OPEN RAIL
STAIRS DN.
Foyer Below
Vaulted M.Bath
SHWR.
LIN.
Opt. Bonus
11⁵ x 11⁹

FIRST FLOOR PLAN

FRENCH DOOR
DECORATIVE COLUMNS
Family Room
19⁰ x 13⁰
Breakfast
Kitchen
DW.
RANGE
REF.
PANT.
FPL.
DECORATIVE COLUMNS
Pwdr.
Garage
19⁵ x 21³
STAIRS DN.
STAIRS UP
COATS
Dining Room
11⁵ x 11⁰
Two Story Foyer
DECORATIVE COLUMN
OPEN RAIL
Study
11⁵ x 11⁰
Covered Porch

copyright © 2002 frank betz associates, inc.

Rear Elevation

Plan number: FSFB02-3671	
Bedrooms: 3	
Baths: 2.5	
Width: 46'-4"	
Depth: 35'-0"	
Main Level:	1019 sq ft
Upper Level:	933 sq ft
Living Area:	1952 sq ft
Opt. Bonus Room	153 sq ft
PRICE CODE: C	

© Frank Betz Associates, Inc.

SECOND FLOOR PLAN

TRAY CEILING
Master Suite 16⁰ x 13⁰
RADIUS WINDOW
Vaulted M.Bath
SHWR.
LINEN
W.i.c.
Foyer Below
OPEN RAIL
STAIRS DN.
Laund.
LIN.
STAIRS UP
Recreation Room 17⁵ x 13⁰
OPEN RAIL
Bath
Bedroom 2 10⁷ x 11³
Bedroom 3 12⁵ x 10⁷
W.i.c.
W.i.c.

CHESNEY

DESIGN NOTES | Brilliant use of space and careful planning is found in the Chesney – a design that gives you usable space without taking away volume and openness. The family room has the higher ceiling and transom windows that are in high demand today. But rather than taking up the entire second story, it is designed with a step-up family recreation area above. The result: an open and roomy main floor and functional space on the second floor. As an added bonus, the laundry is incorporated into the upper level, accessible to all bedrooms.

Plan number: FSFB02-3750	
Bedrooms: 3	
Baths: 2.5	
Width: 40'-0"	
Depth: 38'-4"	
Main Level:	908 sq ft
Upper Level:	1187 sq ft
Living Area:	2095 sq ft
PRICE CODE: **C**	

2'-0" TRANSOM ABOVE
2'-0" TRANSOM ABOVE
FRENCH DOORS
FPL.
RANGE
DW.
SERVING BAR
Kitchen
Breakfast
Family Room 17⁵ x 13⁰
10'-11" HIGH CEILING
REF.
PANT.
COATS
Pwdr.
STAIRS DN.
Dining Room 12³ x 11⁰
DECORATIVE COLUMN
OPEN RAIL
STAIRS UP
Garage 19⁵ x 22²
Two Story Foyer
COVERED ENTRY
copyright © 2002 frank betz associates, inc.

FIRST FLOOR PLAN

Rear Elevation

TO ORDER PLANS CALL TOLL FREE 888-717-3003

© Frank Betz Associates, Inc.

HOLLISTER

DESIGN NOTES | The Hollister is a pleasant combination of traditional and present-day design elements. A time-honored brick façade takes you for a walk down memory lane, but a two-story family room gives the grandeur that you want from your new home. A study and a dining room border the foyer, while tray and vaulted ceilings beautify the master suite. A bay window in the breakfast area provides an ideal spot for morning coffee. Optional bonus space is available on the upper floor, giving the opportunity for a fifth bedroom, craft room or children's recreation area.

SECOND FLOOR PLAN

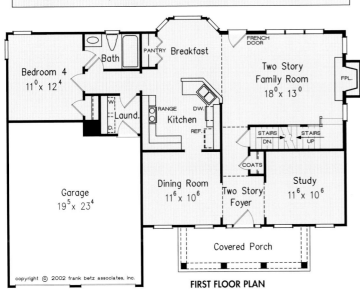

FIRST FLOOR PLAN

copyright © 2002 frank betz associates, inc.

Rear Elevation

Plan number: FSFB02-3736
Bedrooms: 4
Baths: 3
Width: 52'-4"
Depth: 38'-6"
Main Level: 1134 sq ft
Upper Level: 1001 sq ft
Living Area: 2135 sq ft
Opt. Bonus Room 158 sq ft
PRICE CODE: E

© Frank Betz Associates, Inc.

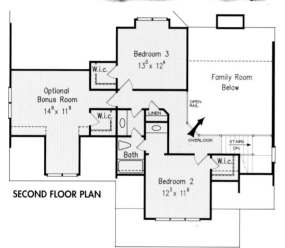

SECOND FLOOR PLAN

Bedroom 3
13⁰ x 12⁴

W.i.c.

Optional
Bonus Room
14⁹ x 11⁹

W.i.c.

LINEN

Bath

OVERLOOK

OPEN
RAIL

Family Room
Below

STAIRS
DN.

W.i.c.

Bedroom 2
12³ x 11⁶

PASADENA

DESIGN NOTES | Charm and character abound from the façade of the Pasadena with its tapered architectural columns and carriage doors. Inside, the master suite is tucked away on the rear of the main level, giving the homeowner a peaceful place to unwind. An art niche is situated in the breakfast area, providing the perfect spot for a favorite art piece or floral arrangement. The kitchen is complete with a large island, making mealtime easier. Upstairs, an optional bonus room has been made available that can be used as the homeowner wishes – a playroom, home office, or fitness room are all fantastic options.

FIRST FLOOR PLAN

TRAY CEILING

Master Suite
17⁰ x 13³

W.i.c.

LINEN

FRENCH DOOR

FRENCH DOOR

Vaulted
M. Bath

K.S.

SEAT
SHWR.

RADIUS
WINDOW

COATS

NICHE

Breakfast

FRENCH DOOR

FPL.

Vaulted
Family Room
16⁰ x 19²

Garage
19⁹ x 19⁹

ISLAND

RANGE

D.W.

Kitchen

REF.

PANT.

copyright © 2002 frank betz associates, inc.

OPEN RAIL

STAIRS
DN.

STAIRS
UP

Dining Room
14⁹ x 12⁰

Foyer

Pdr.

Covered Porch

Plan number: FSFB02-3756	
Bedrooms: 3	
Baths: 2.5	
Width: 50'-0"	
Depth: 57'-0"	
Main Level:	1561 sq ft
Upper Level:	578 sq ft
Living Area:	2139 sq ft
Opt. Bonus Room	274 sq ft
PRICE CODE: **E**	

Rear Elevation

TO ORDER PLANS CALL TOLL FREE 888-717-3003

© Frank Betz Associates, Inc.

Southern Living
Design Collection

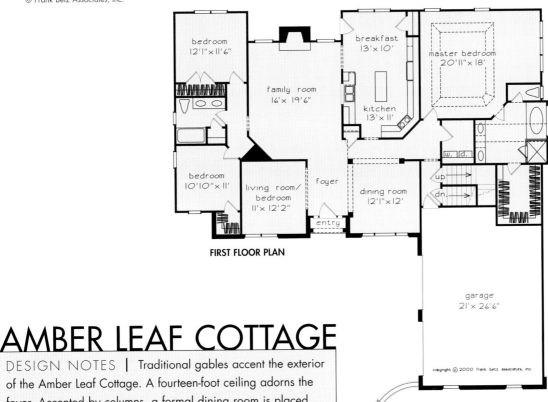

bedroom
12'1" × 11'6"

family room
16' × 19'6"

breakfast
13' × 10'

master bedroom
20'11" × 18'

kitchen
13' × 11'

bedroom
10'10" × 11'

living room/
bedroom
11' × 12'2"

foyer

dining room
12'1" × 12'

w. ld.

up

dn.

FIRST FLOOR PLAN

entry

garage
21' × 26'6"

copyright © 2000 frank betz associates, inc.

dn.

bonus room
11' × 18'6"

OPT. SECOND FLOOR PLAN

AMBER LEAF COTTAGE

DESIGN NOTES | Traditional gables accent the exterior of the Amber Leaf Cottage. A fourteen-foot ceiling adorns the foyer. Accented by columns, a formal dining room is placed conveniently near the kitchen and an expansive great room for entertaining. The kitchen features a large island and generously sized breakfast area, perfect for family gatherings. A grand master bedroom is graced with a tray ceiling and large sitting area which provides a personal retreat after a busy day. The master bath is luxuriously complete with double vanities, a separate shower and large walk-in closet. Two bedrooms share a bath in the right wing of the home. Upstairs, a large bonus area with its own bath creates the perfect teen or in-law suite.

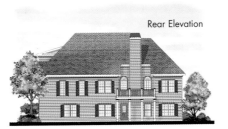

Rear Elevation

Plan number:	FSFB02-3530
Bedrooms:	4
Baths:	3
Width:	64'-6"
Depth:	63'-0"
Main Level:	2195 sq ft
Living Area:	2195 sq ft
Opt. Second Floor	378 sq ft

PRICE CODE: **E**

© Frank Betz Associates, Inc.

BRODERICK

DESIGN NOTES | Function and style...this fresh and innovative design has the functionality to accommodate busy lives and the special touches that give it style! The kitchen adjoins a bright and cheery vaulted breakfast area. Transom windows allow natural light to pour into the family room. A sitting room with a fireplace is situated in the master suite giving homeowners the perfect spot to curl up with a good book. The living room can be easily converted into a fourth bedroom. Additional space is available on the upper level, providing the possibility for a fifth bedroom and a bonus room to be used as you wish.

OPT. SECOND FLOOR PLAN

FIRST FLOOR PLAN

Rear Elevation

Plan number: FSFB02-3566

Bedrooms: 5
Baths: 3.5
Width: 63'-0"
Depth: 72'-4"
Main Level: 2426 sq ft
Living Area: 2426 sq ft
Opt. Second Floor 767 sq ft

PRICE CODE: **D**

MORNINGSIDE

DESIGN NOTES | Homes with character are always welcome in a neighborhood. Our Morningside is a beautiful example of new design with traditional details. Its appeal is timeless. Guests stepping into the two-story foyer immediately sense the spaciousness of the house. Architectural features include arched openings and columns framing the dining and family rooms. A bay with large windows brings light into the living room. The family room, kitchen, and breakfast room are grouped together for convenience. The family room's 2 story ceiling accentuates the open feeling. A spacious master bedroom is on the first floor, with three additional bedrooms and two baths upstairs.

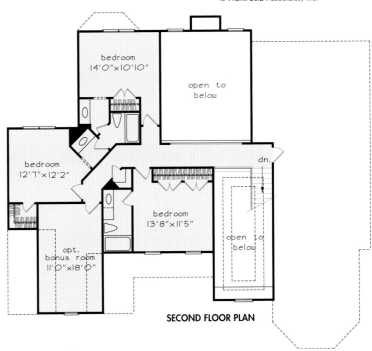

SECOND FLOOR PLAN

- bedroom 14'0"×10'10"
- open to below
- bedroom 12'7"×12'2"
- bedroom 13'8"×11'5"
- opt. bonus room 11'0"×18'0"
- open to below
- dn.

FIRST FLOOR PLAN

- breakfast 10'7"×9'6"
- kitchen 14'0"×11'11"
- family room 15'5"×18'1"
- garage 21'5"×21'8"
- dining 13'8"×13'9"
- master bedroom 16'5"×22'0"
- foyer
- up
- dn.
- living 14'5"×16'0"
- w   d

copyright © 1999 frank betz associates, inc.

Rear Elevation

Plan number: FSFB02-1257	
Bedrooms:	4
Baths:	3.5
Width:	63'-0"
Depth:	56'-0"
Main Level:	2074 sq ft
Upper Level:	896 sq ft
Living Area:	2970 sq ft
Opt. Bonus Room	209 sq ft
PRICE CODE:	**F**

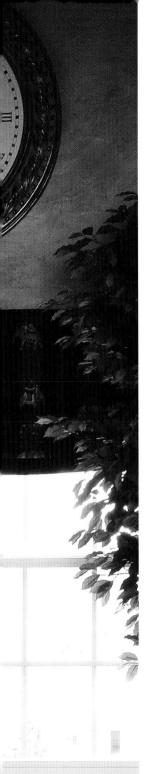

LOFT
SPACES

Lofts enhance home plans with a spirit of fun. Spatial links to the upper and lower rooms are vital connections within the home. A flex space that is as comfortable as a conversation spot as it is a study area, the loft holds an infinite capacity for change as the family's needs evolve. The Hopkins [Left] plan provides a very functional floor plan with many opportunities for change as lifestyles evolve. On the main floor, the flexible den converts to Bedroom Four, and ties the public and private realms together. Upstairs, an expansive balcony hall overlooks the family room and links the secondary bedrooms with an open-rail staircase that could be extended to the loft space. The added space will visually increase the dimensions of the home, and add to the function and livability of the entire plan. ▪

Left | This loft with faux finished walls and interesting ceiling is the perfect home office.

© Frank Betz Associates, Inc.

BREWSTER

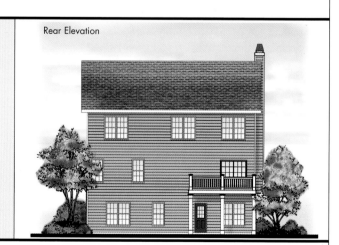

Classic red brick and white stucco accents combine to make a stunning façade on the Brewster. Alternate design options give the homeowner plenty of choice on how they want their finished product to be. An optional bonus room upstairs makes the perfect playroom or exercise area. The impressive dining room has a rare two-story ceiling, however an optional loft or fourth bedroom can be easily incorporated by opting to utilize this space. Vaulted ceilings and a decorative plant shelf make the main floor of this design interesting and dimensional. The laundry room and a handy coat closet are strategically placed just off the garage.

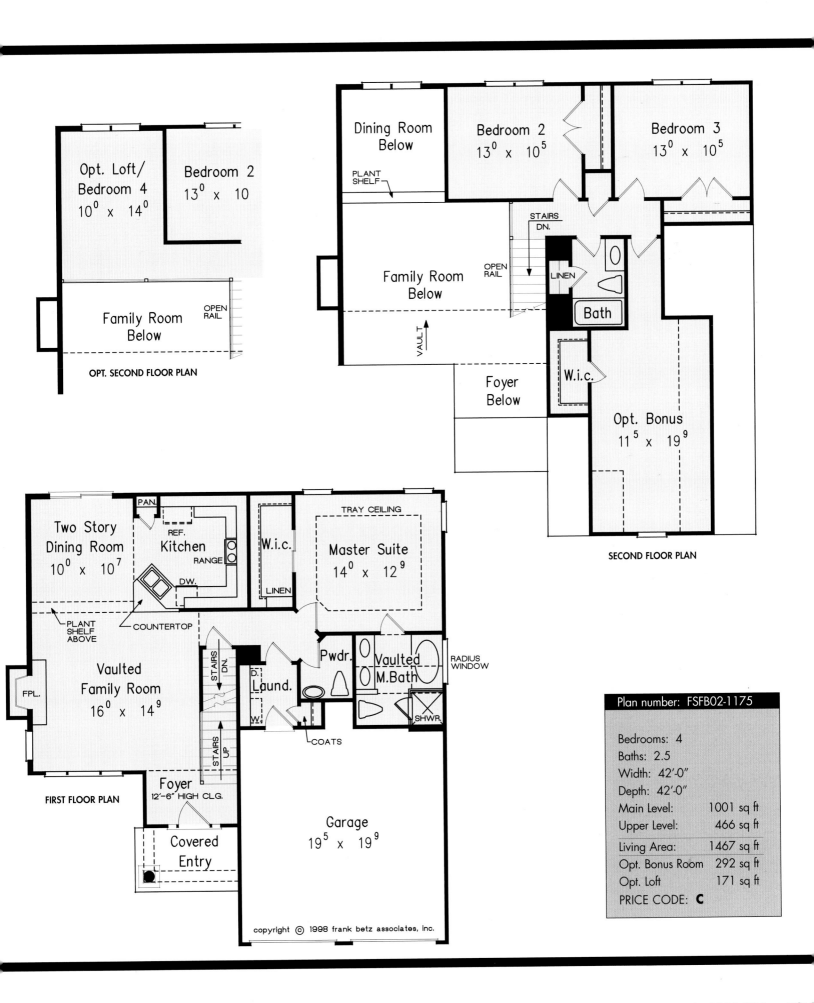

Opt. Loft/
Bedroom 4
10^0 x 14^0

Bedroom 2
13^0 x 10

Family Room
Below

OPEN RAIL

OPT. SECOND FLOOR PLAN

Dining Room
Below

PLANT SHELF

Bedroom 2
13^0 x 10^5

Bedroom 3
13^0 x 10^5

STAIRS DN.

OPEN RAIL

LINEN

Bath

Family Room
Below

VAULT

W.i.c.

Foyer
Below

Opt. Bonus
11^5 x 19^9

SECOND FLOOR PLAN

PAN.

REF.
Kitchen
RANGE

Two Story
Dining Room
10^0 x 10^7

PLANT SHELF ABOVE

COUNTERTOP

DW.

W.i.c.

LINEN

TRAY CEILING

Master Suite
14^0 x 12^9

FPL.

Vaulted
Family Room
16^0 x 14^9

STAIRS DN.

STAIRS UP

D.
W.

Laund.

COATS

Pwdr.

Vaulted
M.Bath

RADIUS WINDOW

SHWR.

Foyer
12'-6" HIGH CLG.

FIRST FLOOR PLAN

Covered
Entry

Garage
19^5 x 19^9

copyright © 1998 frank betz associates, inc.

Plan number: FSFB02-1175	
Bedrooms:	4
Baths:	2.5
Width:	42'-0"
Depth:	42'-0"
Main Level:	1001 sq ft
Upper Level:	466 sq ft
Living Area:	1467 sq ft
Opt. Bonus Room	292 sq ft
Opt. Loft	171 sq ft
PRICE CODE:	**C**

LAKESHORE

Every neighborhood welcomes a home that brings the warmth and friendliness that the Lakeshore does with its brick and siding exterior. Thoughtful design and layout is apparent inside. A large island, double ovens and a butler's pantry take the work out of entertaining. Upstairs, two secondary bedrooms share a divided bath, while the master suite features a large private bath, generous walk-in closet and views to the backyard. There is also a secluded bonus room that overlooks the family room.

Rear Elevation

SECOND FLOOR PLAN

Opt. Bonus Room 12⁰ x 20⁴

Family Room Below

RADIUS WINDOW
RADIUS WINDOW
RADIUS WINDOW

TRAY CEILING

Master Suite 18⁰ x 13⁰

W.i.c
LINEN
PLANT SHELF

OPEN RAIL
OVERLOOK

OPEN RAIL
STAIRS DN.
STAIRS DN.
OPEN RAIL
OVERLOOK

FRENCH DRS.

SHWR.
Vaulted M.Bath
K.S.
RADIUS WINDOW

Foyer Below

Bedroom 2 12⁰ x 13⁴
LIN.
Bath
Bedroom 3 11² x 13⁵
W.i.c.

FIRST FLOOR PLAN

FPL.

Bedroom 4/ Den 12⁰ x 11²

Two Story Family Room 15⁰ x 18⁰

FRENCH DOOR
D.W.
Breakfast
ISLAND
REF.
Kitchen
SURF. UNIT
OVENS
PANTRY
Laun.
W
D

W.i.c.
Bath
LINEN
STAIRS DN.
COATS
BUTLERS PANTRY

Vaulted Living Room 12⁰ x 12³
STAIRS UP
Two Story Foyer
Dining Room 12⁰ x 13⁴
Garage 20⁵ x 22²

Covered Porch

copyright © 2002 frank betz associates, inc.

Plan number: FSFB02-3752

Bedrooms: 4
Baths: 3
Width: 55'-0"
Depth: 47'-10"
Main Level: 1483 sq ft
Upper Level: 1024 sq ft
Living Area: 2507 sq ft
Opt. Bonus Room 252 sq ft

PRICE CODE: **E**

OAK KNOLL

This design was created to give homeowners living spaces that are supplementary to the traditional rooms found in most plans. The master suite is enhanced by a private sitting area with views overlooking the backyard. Just off the breakfast area is a bright and sunny keeping room with a radius window. Kids will appreciate having a private spot to study in the loft designed into the upper level of this home. It features a built-in media center equipped for a computer. Optional bonus space is also available on the second floor, creating extra space for a home gym, office or craft room.

Rear Elevation

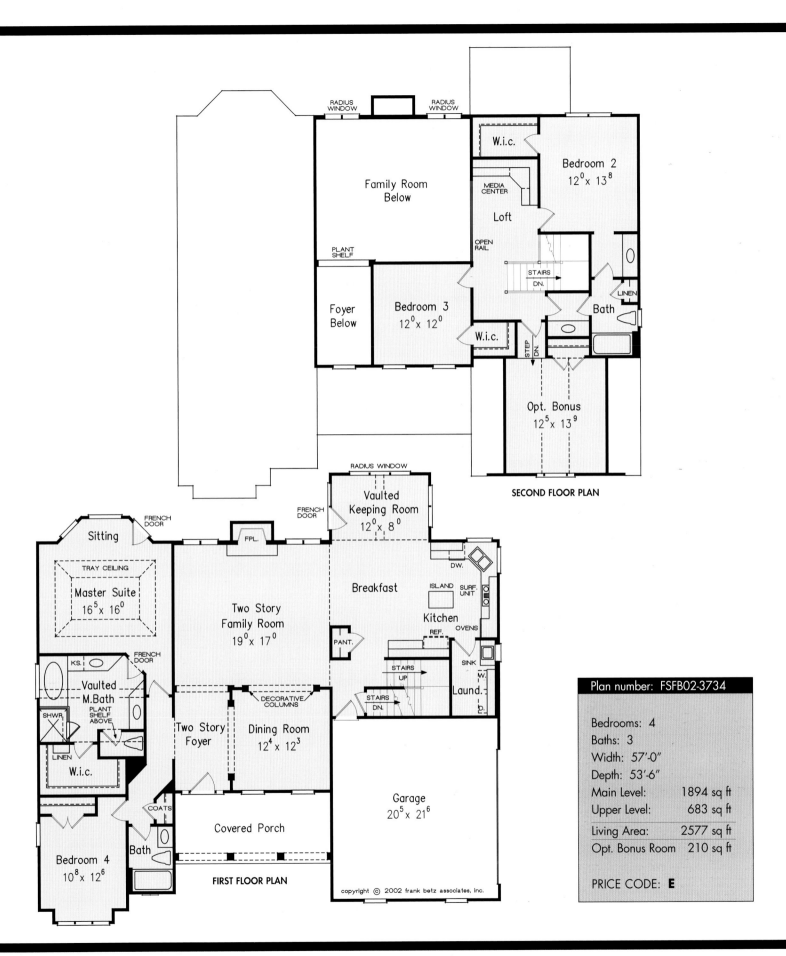

SECOND FLOOR PLAN

Radius Window

Family Room Below

W.i.c.

Bedroom 2
12^0 x 13^8

Media Center

Loft

Open Rail

Plant Shelf

Foyer Below

Bedroom 3
12^0 x 12^0

Stairs Dn.

Step Dn.

W.i.c.

Linen

Bath

Opt. Bonus
12^5 x 13^9

FIRST FLOOR PLAN

French Door

Sitting

Tray Ceiling

Master Suite
16^5 x 16^0

Radius Window

FPL.

French Door

Vaulted Keeping Room
12^0 x 8^0

DW.

French Door

Breakfast

Island

Surf. Unit

Two Story Family Room
19^0 x 17^0

Kitchen

Ovens

Ref.

KS.

Vaulted M.Bath

Plant Shelf Above

Pant.

Stairs Up

Sink

SHWR

Linen

W.i.c.

Decorative Columns

Stairs Dn.

W.

Laund.

Two Story Foyer

Dining Room
12^4 x 12^3

Garage
20^5 x 21^6

Coats

Bedroom 4
10^8 x 12^6

Bath

Covered Porch

copyright © 2002 frank betz associates, inc.

Plan number: FSFB02-3734

Bedrooms: 4
Baths: 3
Width: 57'-0"
Depth: 53'-6"
Main Level: 1894 sq ft
Upper Level: 683 sq ft
Living Area: 2577 sq ft
Opt. Bonus Room 210 sq ft

PRICE CODE: **E**

CANDLER PARK

A covered front porch lends a warm, Southern charm to this elegant home. After a meal in the front dining room, retire to the spacious vaulted family room in the center of the main floor. The kitchen's serving bar and breakfast area are perfect for any morning, with French doors that open onto a second covered porch. A vaulted keeping room adjoins the breakfast and kitchen areas. Upstairs, a loft overlooks the family room, adjoined by bedrooms and a bonus room for a growing family.

Rear Elevation

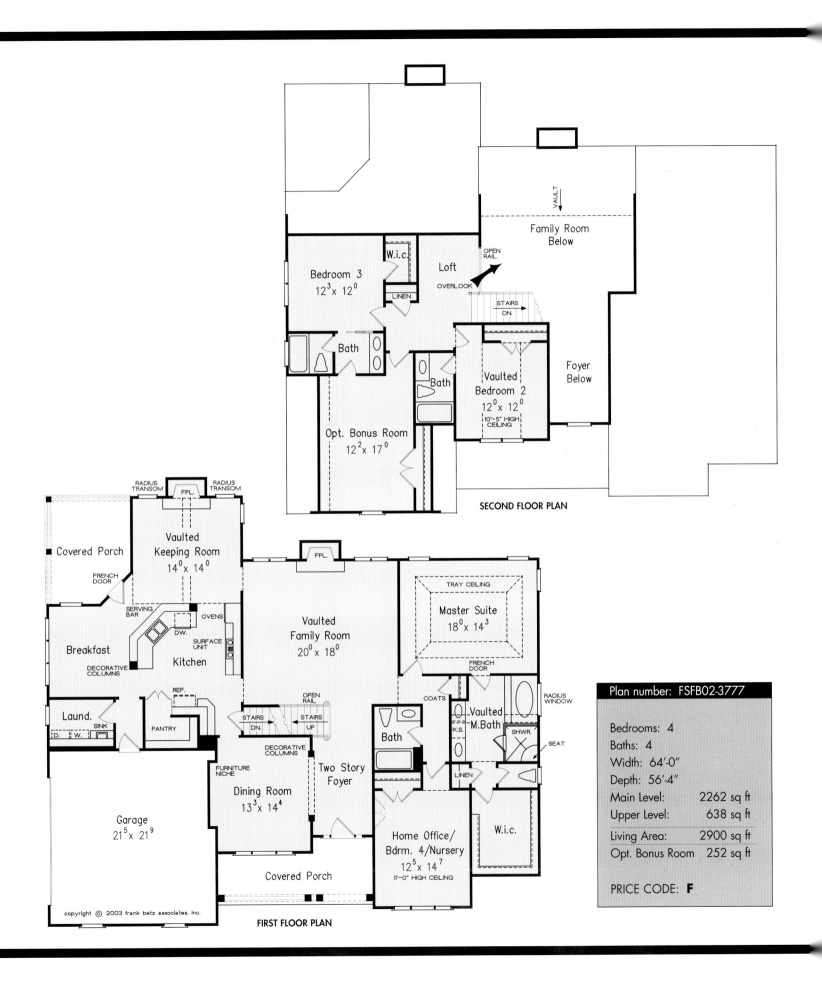

SECOND FLOOR PLAN

Family Room Below

VAULT

Bedroom 3
12³ x 12⁰

W.i.c.

Loft

OPEN RAIL

OVERLOOK

LINEN

STAIRS DN.

Bath

Foyer Below

Opt. Bonus Room
12² x 17⁰

Bath

Vaulted Bedroom 2
12⁰ x 12⁰
10'-5" HIGH CEILING

FIRST FLOOR PLAN

Covered Porch

RADIUS TRANSOM   FPL.   RADIUS TRANSOM

Vaulted Keeping Room
14⁰ x 14⁰

FRENCH DOOR

SERVING BAR

DW.   OVENS

SURFACE UNIT

Breakfast

DECORATIVE COLUMNS

Kitchen

FPL.

Vaulted Family Room
20⁰ x 18⁰

TRAY CEILING

Master Suite
18⁰ x 14³

FRENCH DOOR

RADIUS WINDOW

REF.

OPEN RAIL

COATS

Vaulted M.Bath

Laund.

SINK

D.   W.

PANTRY

STAIRS DN.   STAIRS UP

K.S.

SHWR.

SEAT

FURNITURE NICHE

DECORATIVE COLUMNS

Two Story Foyer

Bath

LINEN

Dining Room
13³ x 14⁴

Garage
21⁵ x 21⁹

Home Office/
Bdrm. 4/Nursery
12⁵ x 14⁷
11'-0" HIGH CEILING

W.i.c.

Covered Porch

copyright © 2003 frank betz associates, inc.

Plan number: FSFB02-3777	
Bedrooms: 4	
Baths: 4	
Width: 64'-0"	
Depth: 56'-4"	
Main Level:	2262 sq ft
Upper Level:	638 sq ft
Living Area:	2900 sq ft
Opt. Bonus Room	252 sq ft
PRICE CODE: **F**	

SECOND FLOOR PLAN

Bedroom 3
12⁰ x 11⁰

Family Room Below

VAULT

W.i.c.
LINEN
Bath

DESK

Loft
11⁰ x 10²

Bedroom 4
12⁸ x 11¹⁰

STAIRS DN.

OVERLOOK

OPEN RAIL

NICHE

Attic

Foyer Below

Opt. Bonus Room
12⁵ x 15⁹

AMELIA

DESIGN NOTES | The Amelia's façade is clean and simple, with a cozy front porch and gabled roofline. Lattice work and stone accents bring a sense of warmth that is echoed inside with a homey floor plan. A bedroom on the main level is also the perfect location for a home office or den. Upstairs, flexible spaces are incorporated giving the homeowners choices on how to use their space. A loft is situated among the bedrooms, making an ideal homework station or lounging area for kids. Optional bonus space is also available, opening up options like a fitness room or media center.

Plan number: FSFB02-3807	
Bedrooms: 4	
Baths: 3	
Width: 54'-0"	
Depth: 48'-0"	
Main Level:	1663 sq ft
Upper Level:	623 sq ft
Living Area:	2286 sq ft
Opt. Bonus Room	211 sq ft
PRICE CODE: **D**	

FIRST FLOOR PLAN

TRAY CEILING

Master Suite
13⁰ x 17⁰

RADIUS WINDOW

FPL.

RADIUS WINDOW

FRENCH DOOR

Breakfast

Bedroom 2
12² x 11⁰

SERVING BAR

Vaulted Family Room
16⁰ x 18⁰

Kitchen

DW.

Bath

REF.

FRENCH DOOR

RADIUS WINDOW

Vaulted M.Bath

RANGE

PANT.

COATS

Laund.
W. D.

SHWR.

LINEN

PLANT SHELF ABOVE

W.i.c.

STAIRS DN.

STAIRS UP

Two Story Foyer

Dining Room
11⁰ x 13⁸

Garage
20⁵ x 20⁸

Covered Porch

copyright © 2003 frank betz associates, inc.

Rear Elevation

TO ORDER PLANS CALL TOLL FREE 888-717-3003

© Frank Betz Associates, Inc.

LULLWATER

DESIGN NOTES | The Lullwater has a friendly façade with its cheery dormers, front porch and stone accents. A vaulted foyer makes the entry way bright and welcoming. The dining room is offset with decorative columns. Radius windows border the fireplace in the family room, creating a dramatic backdrop. Bedroom four has a very private location making it an ideal guest suite or home office. A loft has been incorporated into the second floor of the home, with many optional uses. This area can be used as a children's retreat, workstation, or den.

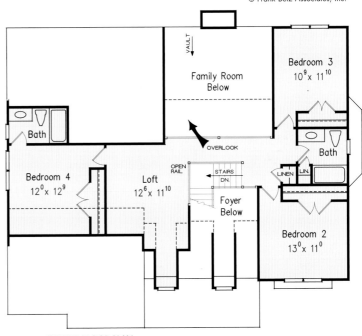

SECOND FLOOR PLAN

Family Room Below

Bedroom 3
10^9 x 11^{10}

Bath

Bath

Bedroom 4
12^0 x 12^9

Loft
12^6 x 11^{10}

OVERLOOK

OPEN RAIL

STAIRS DN.

Foyer Below

LINEN LIN

Bedroom 2
13^0 x 11^0

VAULT

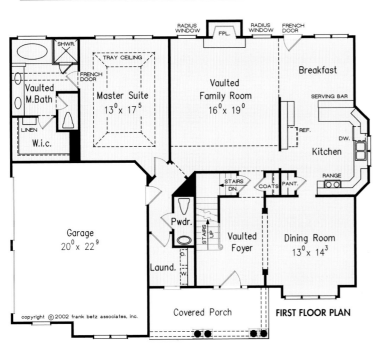

FIRST FLOOR PLAN

RADIUS WINDOW — FPL. — RADIUS WINDOW — FRENCH DOOR

Vaulted M.Bath

SHWR.

FRENCH DOOR

TRAY CEILING

Master Suite
13^0 x 17^5

Vaulted Family Room
16^0 x 19^0

Breakfast

SERVING BAR

REF.

LINEN

W.i.c.

Garage
20^0 x 22^9

STAIRS DN.

COATS

PANT.

Kitchen

DW.

RANGE

Pwdr.

STAIRS UP

Vaulted Foyer

Dining Room
13^0 x 14^3

Laund.

Covered Porch

copyright © 2002 frank betz associates, inc.

Rear Elevation

Plan number: FSFB02-3684

Bedrooms: 4

Baths: 3.5

Width: 53'-0"

Depth: 45'-4"

Main Level: 1509 sq ft

Upper Level: 929 sq ft

Living Area: 2438 sq ft

PRICE CODE: D

© Frank Betz Associates, Inc.

DUNLEAVY

DESIGN NOTES | The exterior combination of brick and siding has stood the test of time. They are as welcomed today as they were in the neighborhoods of yesterday. The Dunleavy – with its traditional exterior – has many modern features inside that will please today's homeowner. A decorative art niche enhances the already impressive two-story foyer. An inviting keeping room is situated just beyond the breakfast area, giving the family a comfortable place to gather. Upstairs, a children's retreat is nestled among the second floor bedrooms. This space is the ideal location for children to do homework, use the computer, and play.

SECOND FLOOR PLAN

- Bedroom 2 — 13⁰ x 12⁰
- Children's Retreat — 12⁵ x 10⁷
- Bedroom 4 — 11⁰ x 11⁸
- Bedroom 3 — 10⁸ x 12⁰
- Family Room Below
- Foyer Below
- W.i.c.
- Open Rail / Niche / Stairs Dn / Overlook
- Linen / Bath / Plant Shelf

Plan number: FSFB02-3728

Bedrooms: 4

Baths: 2.5

Width: 50'-0"

Depth: 54'-0"

Main Level: 1618 sq ft

Upper Level: 848 sq ft

Living Area: 2466 sq ft

PRICE CODE: **D**

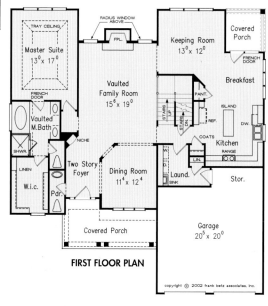

FIRST FLOOR PLAN

- Master Suite — 13⁰ x 17⁰ (Tray Ceiling)
- Vaulted Family Room — 15⁶ x 19⁰
- Keeping Room — 13⁰ x 12⁰
- Covered Porch
- Vaulted M.Bath
- Breakfast
- Kitchen
- Two Story Foyer
- Dining Room — 11⁴ x 12⁴
- Garage — 20⁵ x 20⁰
- Covered Porch
- Radius Window Above / FPL / French Door / Island / Pant. / Ref. / Dw. / Range / Coats / Lin. / Laund. / Sink / Stor. / Niche / Linen / W.i.c. / Pdr. / Shwr.

copyright © 2002 frank betz associates, inc.

Rear Elevation

BROOKWOOD PARK

DESIGN NOTES | The Brookwood Park's impressive façade features timber-accented gable and carriage doors on the garage. Nature enthusiasts will love the screened porch just off the breakfast area. The main floor bedroom can be used as a study or den. A distinctive amenity in this design is the large loft on the upper floor. Situated among the secondary bedrooms, this area is the ideal location for a children's retreat or homework station. Careful incorporation of unique design elements gives this home personality, like arched openings, decorative columns and built-in cabinetry.

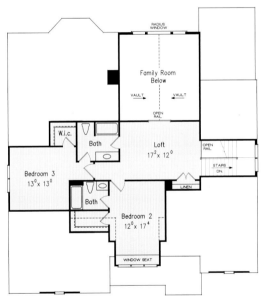

SECOND FLOOR PLAN

FIRST FLOOR PLAN

Rear Elevation

Plan number: FSFB02-3793

Bedrooms: 4

Baths: 4

Width: 54'-0"

Depth: 59'-6"

Main Level: 2123 sq ft

Upper Level: 878 sq ft

Living Area: 3001 sq ft

PRICE CODE: E

Southern Living
Design Collection

© Frank Betz Associates, Inc.

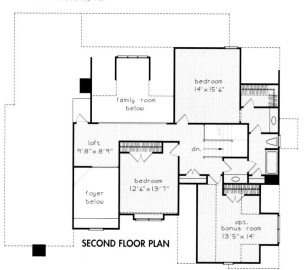

SECOND FLOOR PLAN

- family room below
- bedroom 14' x 15'6"
- loft 9'8" x 8'9"
- dn.
- foyer below
- bedroom 12'6" x 13'7"
- opt. bonus room 13'5" x 14'

STONECREST

DESIGN NOTES | Board-and-batten siding, stone and an arched, covered entry come together to create a warm exterior for the Stonecrest. Inside, a formal living room rests on the left, featuring a coffered ceiling for a dramatic effect. The grand, two-story foyer is accented with a creative art niche. A large dining room is defined by traditional columns. A large kitchen flows comfortably into a generous breakfast room providing ample space for family gatherings or social functions. A grand master bedroom is adorned with a tray ceiling and luxurious master bath, functionally designed with double vanities, a garden tub, separate shower and walk-in closet. Large optional bonus space provides the potential for a fourth bedroom or recreational space.

Plan number: FSFB02-3494	
Bedrooms:	3
Baths:	2.5
Width:	63'-6"
Depth:	53'-0"
Main Level:	2093 sq ft
Upper Level:	923 sq ft
Living Area:	3016 sq ft
Opt. Bonus Room	264 sq ft
PRICE CODE:	F

- covered porch
- breakfast 11'5" x 8'
- master bedroom 14' x 18'10"
- family room 17'8" x 15'6"
- kitchen 22'5" x 15'5"
- up
- dn
- living 14'5" x 12'
- foyer
- dining 12'2" x 14'
- garage 21'5" x 21'8"
- entry

FIRST FLOOR PLAN

copyright © 2000 frank betz associates, inc.

Rear Elevation

TO ORDER PLANS CALL TOLL FREE 888-717-3003

© Frank Betz Associates, Inc.

INMAN PARK

DESIGN NOTES | Innovative and refreshing – the Inman Park includes some of today's hottest design trends. The master suite includes a luxurious private sitting area, and his and her closets with a dressing mirror. The family room brings excitement to the main floor with bright transom windows, a dramatic coffered ceiling and stylish built-in cabinetry. A vaulted keeping room off the gourmet kitchen provides an additional warm and casual spot to lounge. Upstairs, a desk is situated in the loft area making the ideal place for kids to do homework or use the computer.

SECOND FLOOR PLAN

FIRST FLOOR PLAN

copyright © 2003 frank betz associates, inc.

Rear Elevation

Plan number: FSFB02-3791

Bedrooms: 5
Baths: 4
Width: 54'-0"
Depth: 66'-0"
Main Level: 2373 sq ft
Upper Level: 976 sq ft
Living Area: 3349 sq ft

PRICE CODE: F

The Covington Ridge [page 49] features mixed elements—brick, siding and stone—to create a textured elevation with a contempary flair.

From top left to bottom right | With light-stained floors and mint walls, this room has a truly modern feel.

A deep tray ceiling and gold walls create a warm, cozy master retreat.

Lots of space and volume make this living room the center of the home.

A built-in work station is the perfect amenity for today's busy lifestyles.

An inviting breakfast bar is the perfect place for a meal or snack.

The black, distressed finish on a wine cabinet provides a lively contrast to the mint green walls.

The Gastonia is charming and quaint when viewed from the street, this ultra-modern home encompasses a form-follows-function disposition, with open spaces and flexible rooms.

From top left to bottom right | Rich, dark stained cabinets create a warm feel to this spacious kitchen.

Sisal and wicker furniture create a casual feel to this keeping room.

Bright fabrics on a day bed set the tone for this guest space.

Mint green walls provide neutrality for a baby girl or boy.

His and her lavatories along with a make up vanity are nice amenities to any master bath.

Built-in book cases provide ample storage for a family book collection.

PLAN**INDEX**

† Indicates photographed homes not featured in Flexible Spaces. Please visit www.flexiblespaces.com to view full plan details.

CONSTRUCTION DRAWING
INFORMATION

CONSTRUCTION DRAWINGS

Each set of plans from Frank Betz Associates, Inc., will provide you with the necessary information needed to construct a home. The actual number of pages may vary but each set of plans will contain the following information:

1 FRONT ELEVATIONS/DETAILS

All plans include the front elevation at 1/4" or 3/16" scale and the sides and rear elevations at 1/8" scale. The elevations show and note the exterior finished materials of the house.

2 ELEVATIONS/ROOF PLAN

The side and rear elevations are shown at 1/8" scale. The roof plan is a "bird's eye" view showing the roof pitches, overhangs, ridges, valleys and any saddles.

3 FOUNDATION PLAN

Every plan is available with a walk-out style basement (three masonry walls and one wood framed rear wall with windows and doors). The basement plans are a 1/4" scale layout of unfinished spaces showing only the necessary 2 x 6 wood framed load-bearing walls. Crawl foundations and/or slab-on-grade foundations are available for many plans. All foundation types are not available for all plans.

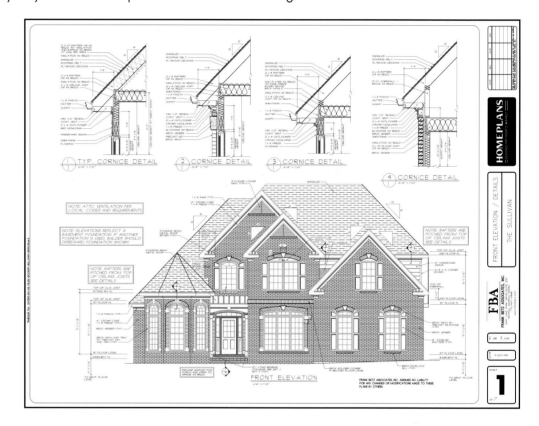

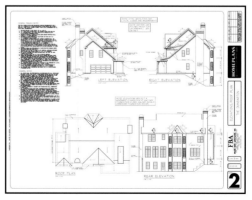

FLOOR PLANS

4 Each plan consists of 1/4" or 3/16" scale floor layouts showing the location of walls, doors, windows, plumbing fixtures, cabinetry, stairs and decorative ceilings. The floor plans are complete with dimensions, notes, door/window sizes and schematic electrical layout.

SECTION(S)

5 The building sections are drawings which take vertical cuts through the house and stairs showing floor, ceiling and roof height information.

KITCHEN AND BATH ELEVATIONS/DETAILS

6 The kitchen and bath elevations show the arrangement and size of each cabinet and other fixtures in the room. These drawings give basic information that can be used to create customized layouts with a cabinet manufacturer. Details are included for many interior and exterior conditions to provide more specific construction information.

FIRST AND SECOND FLOOR FRAMING PLANS

7 The floor framing plans show each floor joist indicating the size, spacing and length. All beams are labeled and sized. All of the joists are counted and coordinated with the material list. Each framing plan sheet includes any framing details that are needed (tray details, connection details, etc.). The framing plans are designed using conventional framing (2 x 8, 2 x 10) or wood I-Joists depending on the span conditions of each individual design.

CEILING JOIST FRAMING

8 The ceiling joist framing plan shows each ceiling joist indicating the size, spacing and length. All beams are labeled and sized. All of the joists are counted and coordinated with the material list.

ROOF FRAMING PLAN

9 The roof framing plan shows each rafter, valley, hip and ridge indicating the size, spacing and length. All beams are labeled and sized. All of the joists are counted and coordinated with the material list.

TYPICAL DETAIL SHEETS

Each plan order includes one set of typical detail sheets that show foundation details, typical wall sections and other framing details. Also included on the detail sheets are miscellaneous interior trim and fireplace details that can be used to customize the home.

ORDERING
INFORMATION

PRICING INFORMATION

Pricing information for our plans can be found in the Plan Index (pages 154-155) and on the Order Form (page 159). Pricing for additional products can also be found on the Order Form. Pricing and plan set information are subject to change without notice.

SHIPPING INFORMATION

Typically we ship our orders the following business day after receipt of order. All plans are shipped via Federal Express 2-day or Overnight. Plans must be shipped to a street address as Federal Express will not deliver to a Post Office Box.

OUR EXCHANGE POLICY

Plans may be returned for a full refund, less applicable restocking fees and shipping charges, by returning the **unopened** package to our office. No returns will be accepted on open boxes, electronic CAD files, or electronic or printed artwork. Plans may be exchanged within 30 days of purchase. Exchanges are subject to price difference and restocking fees.

CODE COMPLIANCE

Our plans are drawn to meet the 2000 International Residential Code for One and Two Family Dwellings and the 2000 International Building Code with the Georgia Amendments. Many states and counties amend the code for their area. Each building department's requirements for a permit may vary. Consult your local building officials to determine the plan, code and site requirements. Frank Betz Associates Homeplans are not stamped by an architect or engineer. Our plans include the drawings typically needed for construction, except site-specific information and heating and cooling requirements. This information, if required, must be provided based on the geographic conditions in your area.

HOW TO ORDER

When placing an order, you may do so online, by mail, fax or phone. To order online visit flexiblespaces.com and follow the directions to the order form. To speak to a customer service representative call 888-717-3003. Orders may be faxed to 770-435-7608 or mailed to Betz Publishing, 2401 Lake Park Drive, Suite 250, Smyrna, Georgia 30080. We accept Visa, Mastercard, American Express and Discover. Orders can also be sent COD for an additional charge. COD orders require certified funds!

IGNORING COPYRIGHT LAWS
CAN BE AN EXPENSIVE MISTAKE

Recent changes in the US copyright laws allow for statutory damages of up to $150,000.00 per incident for copyright infringement involving any of the copyrighted plans found in this publication. The law can be confusing. So, for your own protection, take the time to understand what you can and cannot not do when it comes to house plans. Please call us for more information on copyright laws.

ORDER FORM

BETZ PUBLISHING LLC.
2401 Lake Park Drive, Suite 250
Smyrna, GA 30080
1.888.717.3003 | **www.flexiblespaces.com**

PLAN PRICES*

CODE	8 SETS	REPRODUCIBLE	CAD
A	$ 645.00	$ 720.00	$ 1145.00
B	$ 705.00	$ 780.00	$ 1245.00
C	$ 765.00	$ 840.00	$ 1345.00
D	$ 825.00	$ 900.00	$ 1445.00
E	$ 885.00	$ 960.00	$ 1545.00
F	$ 945.00	$1020.00	$ 1645.00
G	$1005.00	$1080.00	$ 1745.00

Prices subject to change without notice

ADDITIONAL PRODUCTS

Additional Sets . . . .$ 45.00

Additional Foundations*
  slab . . . .$ 125.00
  basement and crawl . . . .$ 175.00
    All foundations are not available for all plans.

Material Workbooks . . . .$ 85.00

Camera-Ready Artwork
  11" x 17" – Color . . . .$ 125.00
  8.5" x 11" – Color . . . .$ 75.00
  8.5" x 11" – Black and White . . . .$ 50.00

SHIPPING

Federal Express 2-Day . . . .$ 25.00

Federal Express Overnight . . . .$ 40.00

C.O.D. (certified funds required) . . . .$ 15.00

For International shipping please call our office.

ORDER FORM

PLAN NUMBER _____

SETS NEEDED

☐ 8 Set Package . . . .$ _____

_____ Number of Sets Reversed

☐ Reproducible . . . .$ _____

☐ CAD . . . .$ _____

☐ Additional Sets @ $ 45.00 each . . . .$ _____

☐ Material Workbook @ $ 85.00 . . . .$ _____

Sub Total _____

Shipping _____

C.O.D. add $ 15.00 _____

Total _____

PAYMENT TYPE (check one)

☐ Visa ☐ Mastercard ☐ American Express ☐ Discover

Credit Card Number_____

Expiration Date_____

Signature _____

Name _____

Company_____

Street_____

City_____ State _____ Zip _____

Daytime Telephone Number_____

Email Address_____

ACKNOWLEDGEMENTS

The homes in this book were inspired by today's changing families. The following builders, Kensington Homes, Inc., Wellstone Development Corp., J.L. Brooks Construction, Lone Star Custom Homes, Inc., Whittemore Homes and Home Traditions, Inc., took our visions and made them a reality. For that we are thankful. It is our hope that these plans will motivate those looking to create the home of their dreams with the flexibility to meet their needs and desires. ▪

FLEXIBLE**SPACES**

A FRANK BETZ ASSOCIATES INC. COLLECTION